P9-CCV-188

FIVE MYTHS ABOUT NUCLEAR WEAPONS

FIVE MYTHS ABOUT NUCLEAR WEAPONS

WARD WILSON

HOUGHTON MIFFLIN HARCOURT

BOSTON   NEW YORK   2013

For information about permission to reproduce selections from this book,
write to Permissions, Houghton Mifflin Harcourt Publishing Company,
215 Park Avenue South, New York, New York 10003.

www.hmhbooks.com

Library of Congress Cataloging-in-Publication Data
Wilson, Ward.
 Five myths about nuclear weapons / Ward Wilson.
   p. cm.
 ISBN 978-0-547-85787-9
 1. Nuclear weapons — Psychological aspects.
 2. Nuclear warfare. 3. Strategy. I. Title.
 U264.W59 2013
 355.02'17 — dc23   2012017322

Book design by Melissa Lotfy

Printed in the United States of America

DOC 10 9 8 7 6 5 4 3 2 1

This book is dedicated to the man on the train.

CONTENTS

I am convinced that to avoid nuclear war it is not sufficient to be afraid of it. It is necessary to be afraid, but it is equally necessary to understand. And the first step in understanding is to recognize that the problem of nuclear war is basically not technical, but human and historical. If we are to avoid destruction, we must first of all understand the human and historical context out of which destruction arises.

— FREEMAN DYSON

FIVE MYTHS ABOUT NUCLEAR WEAPONS

INTRODUCTION

For nearly seventy years, we have lived in fear — even in abject terror — of nuclear weapons. These fears have changed shape and intensity depending on the world situation, but they have never disappeared. At one time, we were so worried about "mutual assured destruction" that schoolchildren practiced hiding under their desks, and homeowners built bomb shelters. Today, though we may be somewhat less concerned about the prospects of wiping out the human race, we still fear nuclear terrorism, nuclear proliferation, and, especially, regimes that seem to be racing to get nuclear weapons, like Iran's.

Nuclear weapons seem to loom over us. We worry that we won't be able to control these dangerous weapons in a crisis. The thought of using nuclear weapons is so unpalatable that for decades we called it "unthinkable." The weapons are the source of deep anxiety and concern. Yet we can't get rid of them because they are — apparently — necessary.

Fear and necessity: the two forces pull in opposite directions. It is a deeply troubling dilemma that echoes throughout the nuclear weapons debate. Consider *Dr. Strangelove,* a darkly comic movie from the early 1960s about a paranoid U.S. Air Force commander who, muttering strange conspiracy theories, sends his bombers to attack Russia without authorization. Despite frantic and bleakly funny efforts to recall the bombers, the movie ends with one mushroom cloud after another rising on the screen. *Dr. Strangelove* still works as a film even today because the actions of the air force general are believable; we can easily imagine someone being driven mad by the responsibility of planning for nuclear war.

In one sense, our concerns are justified. The possibility that nuclear weapons will get used is a clear and present danger. War has been a stubborn and consistent part of human experience for thousands of years. War may be instinctual; it may not. But it is certainly rooted in the deepest parts of human character. These sorts of deep-seated urges can overwhelm common sense. The chances that a large war will one day come and that nuclear weapons will be used if they're available are still disconcertingly high.

Our fears about nuclear weapons have had enormous influence upon U.S. foreign policy and the foreign policies of many other nations. During the Cold War, those fears drove us to engage in an astonishingly expensive arms race; they caused panic during the Cuban missile crisis; they hovered over the proxy wars the United States fought with the Soviet Union. But even though the Cold War has ended, nuclear weapons have not released their hold on our imaginations. They played a leading role in the Bush administration's justification for invading Iraq in 2003; they led Israel to bomb an Iraqi reactor and a Syrian weapons facility; and they may yet lead to violence in Iran.

But what if our thinking about nuclear weapons is flat-out wrong? What if the assumptions that undergirded the Cold War arms race are wrong? What if our military planning and budgeting are based on faulty logic? What if, during the seven decades that have elapsed since atomic weapons were used in anger for the first and only time, we have made our choices based on beliefs that have little foundation in reality and that have been repeatedly contradicted? What if our deep-seated fears are justified, but our decades-old belief that nuclear weapons are necessary is not?

Recently there has been a noticeable shift in attitudes toward nuclear weapons. In 2007, prominent figures of the Cold War — led by George Shultz, William Perry, Henry Kissinger, and Sam Nunn — proclaimed publicly that they supported the goal of "a world free of nuclear weapons," and the announcement was a turning point in the U.S. debate about nuclear security. That 2007 *Wall Street Journal* op-ed "had a transformational effect, fundamentally reconfiguring the positions within the debate on US nuclear policy for the first time in more than half a century."[1] President Barack Obama's speech in Prague and the 2010 Nuclear Posture Review continued the shift.

In the twenty years since the end of the Cold War, new scholarship has been quietly revolutionizing the thinking about nuclear weapons. A careful review of the facts shows that the usefulness of nuclear weapons has been overblown. Inflated claims were made (and kept inflated by Cold War fears) that cannot be substantiated by the history. Much of the thinking of proponents about nuclear weapons is built on myth, misperception, exaggeration, and error. This book lays out those myths, examines the facts, and measures how far the positions of proponents have strayed from reality.

Most opponents of nuclear weapons use horror and moral outrage to make their case. They argue that humanity needs to fundamentally change its nature. But neither emotional anguish nor revolutionary change is necessary in order to imagine solutions to the problem of nuclear weapons. Pragmatic arguments that banish myths and errors with facts from the historical record are sufficient. We do not have to surrender our values, our morals, or our way of living in order to deal sensibly with nuclear weapons. Nuclear weapons are an anomaly, and we can therefore take practical steps to handle them without having to change everything.

A Four-Part Story

Knowledge comes from experience. Our ideas about nuclear weapons have grown out of our experiences with them, limited though those experiences may be. Four key experiences led people to think they understood nuclear weapons; four events coalesced into common knowledge.

This book will reexamine the story of nuclear weapons through its four parts. Call them the shock, the leap, the crisis, and the peace. Each of these four experiences led to the formation of an idea, and each of those four ideas became a foundation stone in the current conventional wisdom. Yet each of these four experiences was misunderstood and misinterpreted. Each of the four foundational ideas they led to are wrong. These errors have become enshrined in myths and have hardened into an orthodoxy that today is as brittle as old bone.

The first part—the shock—covers early decisions to pursue nuclear weapons, and its most important event is the first (and only) use of nuclear weapons in war. The bombing of Hiroshima and Nagasaki and subsequent surrender of Japan was an event that led to a crucial conclusion: nuclear weapons have a unique ability to shock and coerce an opponent.

The second phase, the leap phase, roughly coincides with the 1950s. It covers the growth of both the Soviet and U.S. arsenals and includes a series of technological advances such as the development of hydrogen bombs and the introduction of long-range missiles to carry them. Although there had been doubts about the effectiveness of bombing cities in World War II, by the mid-1950s, there were none. The H-bomb represented, it was believed, a revolution, a quantum leap in the destructiveness, and therefore the decisiveness, of nuclear weapons.

The third part, the crisis, overlaps the others, running from the middle 1950s into the 1970s. But its high point is the early 1960s. Nuclear arsenals grew to extraordinary sizes in this phase, and Cold War tensions spiraled higher and higher as well. The key events, however, were a remarkable string of confrontations between the United States and Soviet Union, any one of which could have led to war. In the event, none of them did. This fact—the avoidance of war despite numerous crises—led people to draw a series of conclusions about nuclear weapons: nuclear deterrence was a strong force; it was robust and reliable; and nuclear weapons —paradoxically—were actually beneficial in a crisis.

The fourth and final part of the story carries us from the 1970s through five decades to the present day. It is a period of relative quiet during which arsenals diminished; for the most part, peace prevailed between nuclear-armed states; and the belief that nuclear arsenals actually promote peace (or maybe even guarantee it) steadily gained adherents. This period also saw the end of the Cold War and a steady de-emphasizing of nuclear weapons. Looking back, people began to say more and more often that nuclear weapons were necessary because they generated and maintained the long peace that stretched from the end of World War II to the present.

Each of these four experiences had a profound impact on ideas about nuclear weapons. Each phase represents an important shift in thinking, and each contributed in different ways to shaping the ideas that make up the orthodoxy that exists today.

Let's consider those four ideas a little more closely. When U.S. officials looked at the prospects for forcing Japan out of the war in the summer of 1945, things appeared pretty bleak. Japan's military had been beaten again and again. Sixty-six cities had been firebombed, to no apparent effect. A submarine blockade was preventing food, economic resources, and military reinforcements from getting in or out of Japan. Starvation loomed. Japan had so little fuel remaining that its fleet was confined to port. Almost all of its experienced pilots had been killed. Yet despite the desperate situation, Japan fought stubbornly on. Then, after the United States' use of only two nuclear weapons, Japan suddenly signaled its willingness to surrender. In his radio broadcast announcing the surrender, the emperor specifically mentioned the atomic bomb as the reason for capitulating.

The obvious conclusion: Nuclear weapons had some remarkable power to coerce an enemy, a power that all those other military means—repeated defeats, economic starvation, even firebombing—could not match. Nuclear weapons, military thinkers and government officials around the world concluded, were unlike any conventional weapon. This weapon could deliver a blow so horrifying that it could coerce surrender when all else could not.

This is the first and most important idea about nuclear weapons. It is the idea on which all the others are built: Nuclear weapons have a psychological power that enables them to coerce and deter when other weapons cannot.

The second episode—the sudden leap upward in destructive power of the H-bomb—made certainty even surer. If it had been possible to question whether atomic weapons were decisive, these new weapons removed all doubts. Hydrogen bombs were "thousands of times" bigger than the bomb that had destroyed Hiroshima. They could devastate even the largest city at a single blow. And there was theoretically no limit to the size of a hydrogen bomb—if you could figure out how to deliver it, you could build a bomb that was a million times more powerful. People took to saying that the hydrogen bomb represented a quantum leap in the power of nuclear weapons.

The third set of events, the part I call the crisis, led to two conclusions. In combination, these two ideas are the most important and dangerous misperceptions there are about nuclear weapons because they have to do with the way we use them. The first conclusion drawn from this period of crisis was that nuclear weapons could be useful in a confrontation. Beginning with the Berlin crisis of 1948, continuing on through the Cuban missile crisis, the Middle East war of 1973, and even to the Gulf War of 1990, nuclear weapons seemed to be effective at persuading opponents to rein in their aggressive actions. When the chips were down, it seemed that the danger of an all-out nuclear war imposed a caution that would not have otherwise existed. Nuclear theorists concluded that it

was possible to manipulate the fear of nuclear war to achieve diplomatic and political objectives. It wasn't necessary to use nuclear
weapons — to actually explode them on the battlefield — for them
to have an impact. Just the mention of them was enough, apparently, to influence events. The experience of the Cold War crises
taught most nuclear theorists that nuclear deterrence was robust
and had a powerful effect on events.

The second lesson that came out of the Cold War was that nuclear weapons seemed to have a calming effect during a crisis. Nuclear weapons didn't seem to incite recklessness or increase the
danger. On the contrary, nuclear weapons apparently led to greater
caution and made resolving the crisis easier. Increasingly, nuclear
strategists assumed that nuclear weapons created something called
crisis stability. All in all, people concluded, nuclear deterrence was
a pretty reliable thing, a useful tool for promoting peace.

The experience of the fourth phase — the long period of peace
among the nuclear powers — seemed to amplify the lessons of the
third. As the years without a major confrontation between the
United States and the Soviet Union stretched out, it came to seem
as if nuclear weapons not only promoted peace in a crisis but actually contributed to peace overall. In a famous article, historian
John Lewis Gaddis argued that the "Long Peace," the sixty-five
years in which no major war was fought either in Europe or between the United States and Russia, was due to the influence of
nuclear weapons.[2] And foreign policy experts from nuclear-armed
states agreed: nuclear weapons were not only beneficial in a crisis
but necessary for peace.

Myths

At least one of the mistaken ideas that were formed during the
story of nuclear weapons was the result of intentional misrepre-
sentation: Japan's leaders purposely misled America's leaders about

why they surrendered. But not all the mistaken ideas about nuclear weapons have such clear-cut origins. Some of the things that are said about these weapons are inexplicable. At least to me. How these ideas transformed from tentative hypotheses to enduring myths is uncertain. But that they *did* transform from possibility to certainty to myth is undeniable.

Consider the Berlin crisis of 1948 and the mysterious way that the facts seemed to shape-shift after the event. The Berlin blockade was the first major crisis of the nuclear era, and in many ways it set the pattern for the crises that came after it. It illustrates how nuclear theorists, historians, and government officials have — in retrospect — consistently transformed what appear to be nuclear-deterrence failures into successes.

Three years after the end of World War II, in the summer of 1948, tensions were rising between the Soviet Union and its former allies. The United States, Great Britain, and France were forging ahead with rebuilding Germany in ways that the Soviets disagreed with. Frustrations mounted, and when negotiations to resolve the disputes went nowhere, the Soviet Union decided to cut off rail and road access to Berlin. Each of the Allies had been assigned a region of Germany as well as a slice of the capital city to oversee. Berlin, divided into four sectors, lay deep in the Soviet portion — the eastern part — of Germany. On June 24, 1948, Soviet forces refused to allow any highway or train traffic from the western part of Germany into Berlin. Without access to supplies from the western part of Germany, the German civilians in the U.S., British, and French sectors of Berlin would starve. It touched off a crisis. There was talk of war. Eventually, the Western powers figured out a way to supply their three sectors of Berlin by air, and after eleven months, the Soviets relented.

During the crisis, as part of the pressure that the United States brought to bear on the Soviet Union, President Truman ordered that a number of B-29 bombers — the same type of plane that had been used to bomb Hiroshima and Nagasaki — be sent to Great

Britain. News of the redeployment was leaked to the press, and the move was "widely interpreted as a demonstration of resolve."[3] In fact, these bombers could not drop atomic bombs. Only a small number of planes had been specially modified to do so, and those were still in the United States. But at the time, what people saw was the possibility of nuclear war. In any event, the redeployment did not seem to have a significant impact on the crisis. The blockade continued for eleven more months, and there is little reason to believe the redeployment affected the final outcome.[4]

As one historian summarized the general reaction in Washington, "In the summer of 1948, American statesmen doubted that the B-29 deployment contributed directly to settlement of the Berlin Blockade crisis." But then a funny thing happened: "as time hazed over the particulars of this episode, they came to believe that atomic arms could be instruments of 'force without war.'" They came to believe, despite the evidence and despite the earlier conclusion they had drawn, that the nuclear weapons had, in fact, played an important part in resolving the crisis. It's not exactly clear what people thought the nuclear weapons had done, but as time passed, there seemed to be a growing sense in Washington that having nuclear weapons was vital in a crisis. Within a year, opinions about the usefulness of nuclear weapons for influencing events had flipped. Even though nuclear weapons hadn't seemed to have much effect at the time, U.S. officials assigned an increasingly important role to them in retrospect. When the Korean War broke out two years later, one historian wrote in 1988, "American statesmen and soldiers brought to the Korean War the conviction that atomic arms, if properly employed, could be extremely valuable tools for conflict management."[5]

What happened here? How could the evidence support one conclusion while the beliefs that eventually emerged took the opposite view?[6] Apparently, where nuclear weapons are involved, beliefs are formed by factors other than evidence alone. And the Berlin crisis is not the only case. Other events led to ideas that didn't fit well with the facts. Concepts of nuclear weapons often seem to acquire the qualities of myth while the facts go unattended.

Man is a mythmaker. Recent neuroscience research shows that story is an essential part of how we think and understand. Even where coherent stories do not exist, our brains try to make up plots to fit the facts.[7] Why we make up myths and how we make up myths are questions we have not completely answered. But that we do shape our experience into myths that reinforce our beliefs is beyond question. Despite the scorn with which we sometimes refer to them ("It's just a *myth!*"), myths have the power to shape identity.[8]

Think about the way myths shape national self-images. Patriotic myths have extraordinary longevity and power. For example, U.S. schools have been teaching children for more than two hundred years that the country's first president could not tell a lie. In the United Kingdom, young children learn about a British king who had a magic sword and believed in equality so strongly that he made his knights sit at a round table.

Where nuclear weapons are concerned, a series of powerful myths have shaped our thinking, distancing us from the facts and undermining pragmatic policymaking. Indeed, these myths have shaped history — for the worse.

Apocalypse

We don't think about nuclear war in terms of carefully reasoned analyses; we think about it in grandiose metaphors. The grandest of all are ancient stories of the Apocalypse. Think about that. The average person's conception of nuclear war is as factual as the story about the guy with the winged horse.

Everyone knows what a nuclear war would be like: it would be an apocalypse. We hardly give that concept a second thought. It is a notion that powerfully frames our thinking about nuclear weapons policy, and it is so common that we notice it about as much as the furniture in our living rooms. But doesn't it seem rather odd that so much of the talk about nuclear weapons is infused with ideas and images from a two-thousand-year-old religious book?

Biblical talk about nuclear weapons appeared from the very beginning. James Chadwick, a British scientist observing the first nuclear test explosion, was awestruck and reached for religious imagery to describe what he saw. "A great blinding light lit up the sky and earth as if God himself had appeared among us . . . there came the report of an explosion, sudden and sharp as if the skies had cracked . . . a vision from the Book of Revelation."[9] Air force general Thomas Farrell described it this way: "Thirty seconds after the explosion came, first, the air blast pressing hard against the people and things, to be followed almost immediately by the strong, sustained, awesome roar which warned of doomsday and made us feel that we puny things were blasphemous to dare tamper with the forces heretofore reserved to the Almighty."[10] J. Robert Oppenheimer, the man who led the scientists who developed nuclear weapons in the United States, claimed that what leaped to his mind as he watched that first fireball rise in the night sky were words from the Bhagavad-Gita, "Now I am become Death, the Destroyer of Worlds."[11] Apocalypse was just a natural way to understand nuclear weapons, apparently.[12]

Consider the other popular name we use for nuclear war. We don't call it super-science war. We don't call it mega-death war. We don't even call it by the luridly whimsical coinage of the strategist Herman Kahn: wargasm. The second most popular name for nuclear war is a reference to the hill in Israel that the Bible states will be the site of the Last Battle at the End of Days. When we're not calling nuclear war apocalypse, we call it Armageddon.

The apocalypse appears as religious prophecy and popular myth across cultures and eras. The book of Daniel in the Jewish Bible is apocalyptic; there are apocalyptic prophecies in the Christian book of Revelation; the Koran has apocalyptic suras.[13] The Zoroastrians predicted the end of time, and Norse sagas have a story about a cataclysmic battle between the gods.[14] Apocalyptic writing is not confined to ancient times. The Sibylline oracles were written by different European authors from the third century to the fifth.[15] The apocalyptic Shangqing scripture of Taoism was produced in China in the fourth century. Nostradamus wrote in the 1500s. Apocalyptic writings led to political uprisings in Germany and England in the sixteenth and seventeenth centuries.[16] At the turn of the nineteenth century, millennialists predicted the end of time and the coming of the Lord at midnight of December 31.

The outlines of the various apocalypses are remarkably similar. Typically, there is a world filled with sin and degradation, and a lone group in that evil world that remains pure through devout faith and strict rules of conduct. The central drama is a world-shaking battle or cataclysmic event that causes staggering death and devastation but that the group — because of its faith — survives. What results is a new and better place: a world washed clean of sin. Believers in apocalypse see approaching doom but feel themselves protected by divine power.

People around the globe have felt the pull of apocalypse for thousands of years. Nuclear weapons did not create our feelings about apocalypse, but they seem to have connected with them strongly. Apocalypse is, however, either a myth or a prophecy. It is not fact. Many different peoples at different times and places have fashioned similar stories to meet what is clearly an important psychic need. Nuclear war would be a very concrete reality. It would have specific characteristics and dimensions. In all likelihood, it would be somewhat like other all-out wars from human history, such as the Mongol wars, the Thirty Years' War, the Napoleonic wars, World War I, and World War II.[17] The exact form nuclear war will take is largely unknowable, but it is unlikely to resemble stories about the apocalypse. There will be no cleansing. An all-out nuclear war is far more likely to lead to a period similar to the Dark Ages (call it the Darkest Age) than an apocalypse. A smaller nuclear war would be even less like an apocalypse — inordinately destructive but not a washing clean of everything.

What the widespread apocalypse analogy tells us is that, given the choice between thinking in terms of religious prophecy or cultural myth and delving into the reality of nuclear war, we grabbed the myth with both hands. Our desire to view nuclear war in terms of the Apocalypse isn't motivated by a need to think realistically about nuclear war. And it's not clear that mythical thinking makes policies more sensible. Why does it make sense to think about a twenty-first-century military phenomenon in terms of religious prophecy or cultural myth?

Pragmatism Versus Myth

Using myths as a guide to cultural identity or for metaphysical storytelling seems to work for human beings. At least, we've done it for thousands of years. But using myths as a guide for dealing with practical problems is a formula for difficulty, at the very least. If you were trying to find the cheapest flight to Europe, would it help to read the story of Daedalus and Icarus?

As it turns out, the debate about nuclear weapons since the 1950s illustrates what happens when you use myth instead of pragmatic analysis. For decades, opponents of nuclear weapons argued that because of the danger, we had to admit that we are too warlike, too prone to aggressive behavior, too caught up in the thrill of new weapons. Nuclear weapons are immoral, they said, and only when we changed our hearts and made war impossible would we be safe from complete destruction. The first response to the creation of nuclear weapons was a wave of support for world government.

Proponents of the weapons, however, argued that we were not being realistic. You can't change human nature, they'd say; nuclear weapons are decisive weapons, and as long as our enemies have them, only a fool would advocate giving them up. Even though nuclear weapons are horrible weapons, they said, in a dangerous world, we have to harden our hearts and do what must be done.

These positions became wearyingly familiar over the course of the next sixty years. Philip Bobbitt once wrote that the nuclear weapons debate was like a prehistoric bug trapped in amber: it had obviously been alive once, but it hadn't moved in millions of years.[18] The unchanging nature of this discussion (really, more like two sides talking past each other) is what, in part, has made people feel that the problems associated with nuclear weapons are largely intractable.

What is striking about the debate described above, however, is the extent to which it is not really about nuclear weapons. Both sides, at bottom, are talking about *us*, about human nature. They touch on nuclear weapons but very quickly turn to the inner workings of the human soul. *We* need to be more mindful of morality, say the opponents. It is our flawed and warlike nature that is the problem. No, no, say proponents. *We* need to be more realistic; it is our foolish unwillingness to face the harsh realities of life that gets us in trouble. Both sides imply that the fault is not in our stars, but in ourselves, that we live under the fear of nuclear war. This is as true of Einstein — "Nuclear weapons have changed everything, except our way of thinking" (*we* have failed to change) — as it is of the famously warlike U.S. Air Force general Curtis LeMay — "I think there are many times when it would be most efficient to use nuclear weapons. However, the public opinion in this country and throughout the world throw up their hands in horror when you mention nuclear weapons, just because of the propaganda that's been fed to them"[19] (*we* are too squeamish).

But this way of thinking about nuclear weapons makes no sense. It shows how quickly and strongly myths can tempt us away from the real matters at hand. It is a practical problem. When a rockslide has blocked a road, the best way to clear the rockslide or find a way around it is not to focus on one's character flaws. You wouldn't look at the rocks and say, *The first step to solving this problem, I think, is for me to have a long talk with my therapist.* To solve a practical problem, you examine the situation, evaluate it realistically, and then take concrete steps. Nuclear weapons are not a nature-of-humans problem; they are a practical problem.

Pragmatism is, in part, an insistence on taking the world as it is. It is a philosophy that values experience before everything. There have been large theoretical treatments of nuclear weapons. There have been works of complex logic stuffed full of mathematical formulas. There have been angry polemics full of emotion and unexamined assumptions. There have not been very many pragmatic analyses that focus just on the facts. Now that the Cold War is over and some of the anger and fear have faded, it might be worth taking a careful look at the facts about nuclear weapons. It might make sense to try to look dispassionately at the evidence.

Emotionally, there is an enormous amount at stake. Even if we are inclined to be realistic about nuclear weapons, we also desperately *want* them to keep us safe. The difficulty is not so much the technology involved as the size of our awe and intensity of our desires. As Ludwig Wittgenstein said, "What makes a subject hard to understand — if it's something significant and important — is not that before you can understand it you need to be specially trained in abstruse matters, but the contrast between understanding the subject and what most people *want* to see."[20]

The stakes are high and very real in terms of policy and violence. Consider most Americans' current attitudes toward Iran. Many people seem to believe that if Iran gets nuclear weapons, it will be magically transformed from a middle-sized power of middling significance on the border between Asia and the Middle East into a behemoth that is able to dominate all the states around it. People seem to imagine that nuclear weapons will make Iran much more influential, that they will give it the power to fundamentally change the situation in the Middle East. Every Republican candidate for president in 2012 (save the lone libertarian, Ron Paul) stated flatly that he or she would not allow Iran to develop nuclear weapons. The likelihood of violent bombing raids on Iran by Israel or even the United States increases with every such statement. But the powers imagined for a nuclear Iran are the kinds of powers that mythical implements give, like the winged sandals used by Perseus or Arthur's sword, Excalibur. It doesn't make sense to expect ordinary weapons to have the power of mythical objects. A pragmatic review of the situation in the Middle East would remind all parties involved that nuclear weapons haven't given Israel the power to dominate the Middle East, and they probably won't give Iran that power either. It would be a bad thing for Iran to get nuclear weapons. The more states that have nuclear weapons, the more likely a war involving nuclear-armed states; the greater the possibility of a war involving nuclear-armed states, the greater the possibility of a war in which nuclear weapons are used. Our ideas about nuclear weapons inform policies that matter, that can bring sudden violence on a massive scale.

But even though in the past, the way we approached these questions was flawed, pursuing radical changes might not be sensible either. With so much at stake, there are good reasons to be cautious. A single nuclear weapon can devastate a city in an instant, and the United States and Russia have thousands of nuclear weapons poised to launch at a moment's notice. Nine nations now have nuclear weapons, and worldwide arsenals total more than twenty thousand nuclear warheads.

In a situation in which international calamity could result from a single misstep, sticking with ideas that have worked in the past might seem like simple prudence. Unfortunately, the danger of nuclear weapons cuts both ways: holding on to mistaken ideas simply because they are familiar can also lead to catastrophe. Basing actions on incorrect theories is like wearing glasses with the wrong prescription: everything is blurry, and the real world is almost impossible to perceive. There is something particularly horrifying about watching a person stumbling near a precipice that he cannot see.

A strong case can be made for caution in the area of nuclear weapons. A stronger case can be made for attending to the facts. We should always cast a skeptical eye on theories or speculations that aren't supported by the actual evidence, even if those theories are the ones that make us feel comfortable and safe. Comfortable illusions are as dangerous in their own way as rushing off after every shiny new theory. Facts matter, and in the arena of nuclear weapons, where the danger is so high, real prudence can only be had by taking the facts seriously, no matter how uncomfortable they make us feel.

Five Myths

Much of the orthodox opinion about nuclear weapons (in nuclear-armed states) is based on "realism." Realism takes facts as they are and denies emotional pleas to believe the world is a better place than it really is. From the realist's perspective, nuclear weapons are the most powerful weapons there are, which gives them a central role in international relations. The ability to destroy a city at a single blow gives states the power to punish on an unprecedented scale, which in turn makes nuclear deterrence almost unquestionably effective. The original success of the bombings of Hiroshima and Nagasaki and the subsequent central role of nuclear weapons in the Cold War confirms the existence of a special, awesome "aura" around the weapons. This aura increases their influence and is a crucial part of their political power. Because they have the ability to punish on a massive scale, nuclear weapons make attacks that threaten the existence of nuclear-armed states unthinkable. They therefore assure the survival of states that possess them. They are, in other words, the ultimate insurance.

In the view of proponents, nuclear weapons are essential weapons; they prop up the international order and prevent the recurrence of massive wars like World War II. In their view, while it is nice to think about a world without nuclear weapons, the possibility of actually getting there without fundamental changes in the way international politics is conducted, and even in the way that human beings conduct themselves, is remote.

The assumptions of proponents of nuclear weapons are theoretically sound. Realism has some little-acknowledged flaws, but it is a generally sensible approach to building sound policies. The difficulty with the position of nuclear proponents is not with the framework of their thinking, but with the facts on which their thesis is founded.

We use the term *myth* loosely in our everyday talk. Sometimes we mean *myth* in the strictly anthropological sense: a story embedded in a culture that works to shape and structure beliefs. Sometimes we use it as a simple pejorative for events that aren't true. Sometimes it has a meaning somewhere in between these two. I'm using the term in this same loose way in this book. The myths here are not all like the apocalypse myths; they are not all clearly symbolic stories. Some are errors or mistakes; some are misperceptions. As the historian Geoffrey Blainey said, "The process by which nations evade reality is complicated."[21] But each myth or error is connected with central misconceptions we have about nuclear weapons.

My plan is to go back over each of the four events in the nuclear weapons story—shock, leap, crisis, and peace—reexamine the evidence, and see if the common interpretations line up with the facts. We'll begin with the bombing of Hiroshima and the belief that grew out of it that nuclear weapons have a special power to shock adversaries into surrendering. Next we'll turn to the idea that killing civilians en masse is an effective way to prosecute a war—the lesson that nuclear strategists drew from the quantum leap in power that occurred when the hydrogen bomb was developed. Then we'll look at the crises of the Cold War—particularly the Cuban missile crisis—from which people concluded that nuclear deterrence is a powerful and reliable way to restrain leaders' aggression. The fourth event—the long peace—will come next. This is the experience people point to when they say that nuclear weapons have kept us safe for more than sixty-five years. Finally, I'll look at an idea that is not associated with any particular historical event but that has grown out of the other four — specifically, that there is no alternative to keeping nuclear weapons.

Each of these ideas will be examined and the facts behind it reviewed. It is a remarkable and surprising business. In some cases, it is clear that the facts directly contradict what is generally believed. In other cases, conclusions have been reached that, while not contradicted by the facts, are not supported by them either. In every case, there are clear problems with the general beliefs about nuclear weapons.

This book challenges conventional thinking about nuclear weapons. It raises questions about fundamental issues. You may find that you don't agree with all of the objections raised here. That would not be surprising. People don't usually agree completely on anything having to do with fundamental issues, much less challenges to long-established ideas. But I hope you will come away with the conviction that there are unaddressed problems in the thinking about nuclear weapons, problems that matter. I hope you will feel that some sort of reexamination and rethinking of those ideas is needed.

People look at how little headway has been made over the past sixty-five years in finding sensible policies for dealing with nuclear weapons, and they feel discouraged. The general perception is that we have talked nuclear weapons issues to death and gotten nowhere. But pessimism is unnecessary. The fact is that the essential conversation, the one that will make a difference, is a conversation we have not yet had. We have not yet had a realistic conversation about nuclear weapons. We have talked about the horror and the military stakes; we have told stories very much like myths; we have shouted angrily about morality and survival; but we have never examined the practical problems — the *usefulness* of nuclear weapons — closely or objectively. It is an exciting, engaging, and perhaps even hopeful prospect. After a careful review, we could well draw radically different conclusions about nuclear weapons than thinkers have in the past.

This book attempts to begin that conversation, a conversation centered not on morality or a false realism but on pragmatic questions. We have to put myths aside, get our identity from other stories that don't involve nuclear weapons, and evaluate these weapons realistically. Are nuclear weapons practical, useful, effective? If they are, then we must keep them. Are they not very useful and enormously dangerous? Then we can safely and sensibly change the way we deal with them.

Now that the Cold War is over, it is time for a conversation that is not overwhelmed by fear and visions of extinction. Let us attempt a pragmatic discussion of nuclear weapons, one characterized by clear-eyed investigation, open minds, and the courage to face uncomfortable truths.

NUCLEAR WEAPONS SHOCK AND AWE OPPONENTS

P SYCHOLOGICAL WEAPONS, he called them. Courtly, tall, reserved — Henry L. Stimson was the perfect man to deliver the first authoritative statement by a U.S. government official on the meaning and importance of nuclear weapons. Two years after the war ended, there were still questions about the use of nuclear bombs on Hiroshima and Nagasaki. Had they really been necessary? What did the new weapons mean for the safety of the United States? Did they foretell the doom of mankind? Stimson was now retired, but during the war, he had been the man in Washington most responsible for the bomb project. So it was natural that when establishment insiders were casting about for a respected figure to reassure the public and justify the use of the Bomb, they chose Stimson. The article that appeared in *Harper's Magazine* in February of 1947 under Stimson's signature framed much of the thinking about nuclear weapons for the next sixty years.

The bombings were justified, Stimson said, and as for the weapons, they were not only phenomenally destructive but also unique in their ability to shock opponents into surrendering. As Stimson explained it: "We had developed a weapon of such a revolutionary character that its use against the enemy might well be expected to produce exactly the kind of shock on the Japanese ruling oligarchy which we desired. . . . [T]he atomic bomb was more than a weapon of terrible destruction; it was a psychological weapon."[1]

It made sense. Cities destroyed with ordinary bombs hadn't forced the Germans to surrender, but two cities destroyed with nuclear bombs coerced Japan's leaders into surrendering in a heartbeat. Here is Stimson again:

> Hiroshima was bombed on August 6, and Nagasaki on August 9. These two cities were active working parts of the Japanese war effort. One was an army center; the other was naval and industrial. Hiroshima was the headquarters of the Japanese Army defending southern Japan and was a major military storage and assembly point. Nagasaki was a major seaport and it contained several large industrial plants of great wartime importance. We believed that our attacks had struck cities which must certainly be important to the Japanese military leaders, both Army and Navy, and we waited for a result. We waited one day.[2]

In the years since Stimson wrote this, the belief that nuclear weapons' psychological power is as important as their enormous destructive power — or even more important — has become one of the fundamental tenets of international relations. The notion is repeated again and again in congressional testimony by military men and government experts from the Defense Department. It makes its appearance in scholarly articles and political debates. It is part of our everyday discourse.[3] Nuclear weapons have a special ability to inspire fear. Reliance on this special psychological power is central to the way the world is currently ordered. After all, nuclear deterrence is based on the ability of nuclear weapons to inspire fear, and the leading nations of the world — China, Russia, and the United States — rely on nuclear deterrence for security. And many other nations — European countries, Japan, South Korea, and others — rely on their nuclear allies to extend nuclear deterrence over them.

Hiroshima was the crucial first impression of nuclear weapons. It provided the proof of their psychological impact. If nuclear weapons were a religion, Hiroshima would be the first miracle. Japan's leaders had stubbornly resisted surrender despite a clearly hopeless situation. Suddenly, miraculously, nuclear weapons coerced them.

The case provides not only a measure of nuclear weapons' effectiveness but a metric for comparing them with other types of military power. The United States and its allies employed a number of military means against Japan. A submarine cordon was blockading Japan's home islands, the economy had collapsed, and starvation was looming. But this was not enough to force Japan to surrender. Japan's navy had suffered a series of stunning defeats, leaving American forces unchallenged in the Pacific and able to launch an invasion of the Japanese home islands at any time. But this was not enough to force Japan to surrender. U.S. ground forces had painfully and with enormous loss of life recaptured many of the islands that Japan's army had conquered in the first years of the war. But this was not enough to force Japan to surrender. The U.S. Army Air Forces had been pounding Japanese cities with high explosives and firebombs for five months, and scores of cities had been hit. But this was not enough to force Japan to surrender. It was only when the atomic bombs destroyed Hiroshima and Nagasaki that Japan's leaders decided they had had enough. So nuclear weapons, one might conclude, are more effective than city bombing with conventional bombs, economic blockade, or a string of military defeats. Or all three combined. They are impressively effective military means.

But even though this seems obvious and wholly persuasive and this version of events has been confidently told as fact for more than sixty years, and even though the lessons drawn from this episode have hardened into certain belief, there are problems. Over the past twenty years, new, more detailed evidence has gradually been unearthed in archives in Japan, Russia, and the United States that often starkly contradicts the traditional narrative. The evidence suggests different ways of looking at the events and offers new interpretations that fit the facts just as well. Or better. The more closely you look, the more difficult it is to feel entirely comfortable with the orthodox interpretation of this event. Almost every Japanese official, from the Showa emperor (Hirohito) on down, said after the war that the atomic bombings compelled them to surrender, but there are troubling actions, meeting minutes, and diary accounts that contradict this assumption.

Revisionists

These problems with the traditional account of events have nothing to do with the revisionist school of thinking about Hiroshima, which was founded by historian Gar Alperovitz in 1965, and which has been the subject of angry debate ever since.[4] Alperovitz argued that Japan's leaders wanted to surrender and that the bombings were therefore unnecessary. Obviously, if the bombings weren't necessary to win the war, then bombing Hiroshima and Nagasaki was wrong. In the decades since Alperovitz introduced the argument, many have joined the fray, some denouncing the bombings, others rejoining hotly that the bombings were moral, necessary, and saved lives. Intense, profound emotions are apparently at stake here. In 1995 — *fifty years* after the event — the Smithsonian touched off an angry national debate (that even members of Congress joined in) by planning an exhibit that included critical statements about the bombing.[5]

It is remarkable. How many issues hold a nation's attention for almost half a century? But it doesn't tell us much about nuclear weapons. They show up in the discussion, of course, but the debate is really about something else. It's actually a discussion about the character of the United States. It is about whether the United States was wrong to bomb Hiroshima and Nagasaki, about whether the United States is morally good. The endpoint of the argument is not "And therefore nuclear weapons are [or are not] effective." The revisionists' argument is "So the bombings were not necessary and therefore were wrong." The revisionist debate about Hiroshima matters to people because it is a reflection on the moral standing of the United States.

That debate, however, is irrelevant here. Whether the United States was right or wrong, what Harry Truman knew and why he agreed to go ahead, whether an offer to allow the emperor to remain would have gotten Japan to surrender earlier, why the scientists who had doubts about using the Bomb were ignored, whether lives were saved, whether Japan would have surrendered anyway because of conventional bombing or some other reason — all this is beside the point.

The question here — the *only* question — is whether the bombing of Hiroshima and Nagasaki with new, more powerful bombs forced Japan to surrender. Did it, in other words, *work?* This is a pragmatic investigation, after all. It might seem heartless to ignore the moral issues. Everyone wants to be proud of his country. And clearly, whether the United States was right or wrong to use nuclear weapons matters a great deal to Americans. But the issue of the effectiveness of nuclear weapons will affect hundreds of millions of people around the globe for generations to come.[6]

In this chapter, we'll be taking a purely pragmatic approach to the bombing of Hiroshima and Nagasaki. The question is: Did nuclear weapons work? The half-century-old debate about whether the bombings were right or wrong, what Truman knew, and so forth is outside the scope of this discussion.

Traditional Interpretation

The traditional story unfolds like this: On August 6, the United States drops a nuclear bomb on Hiroshima, devastating the city. Word of the destruction is slow to reach the capital (as most means of communication have been destroyed, and this is an entirely new phenomenon). The emperor soon hears about it, however, and is deeply moved. Back in the United States, President Truman issues a press release announcing that an atomic bomb (as nuclear weapons were then called) was used and threatens "a rain of ruin" on Japan's cities if Japan does not surrender. After three days of inaction, on August 9, Japan's leaders meet to discuss surrender. They talk all day, debating conditions of surrender, but even though the situation is hopeless, the military stubbornly refuses to admit defeat. Even after word arrives during the late morning that Nagasaki has also been bombed with a nuclear weapon, they are still deadlocked. Finally, late that night, a special meeting with the emperor is called and he tells the military that they must surrender because of the Bomb. The emperor then announces the surrender to Japan in a radio broadcast, explaining that the cause of Japan's defeat is the horrible new weapon the United States has invented. In the United States, where people had expected a long and bloody invasion of Japan, the news is greeted with disbelief, gratitude, and joy. The Bomb is regarded as a miracle and dubbed "the winning weapon."

This is the version of events that has been told by most historians for more than sixty-five years.[7]

The lesson people have drawn from this narrative is that the military and psychological power of nuclear weapons is extraordinary. The dramatic destruction of an entire city in the blink of an eye was decisive. While bombing cities with conventional bombs did not force Germany or Japan to surrender (or Great Britain or any number of other countries, for that matter), bombing with nuclear weapons was clearly different. The story of Hiroshima shows —and this is all according to the traditional version of events— that the ability of nuclear weapons to shock and overawe nations is enormous.

This orthodox view of the bombing of Hiroshima and Nagasaki is widely taught and widely believed. The support for this view of history runs deep. But there are four major problems with telling

the story in this way, and, taken together, they significantly undermine the traditional explanation of the Japanese surrender. It is,
perhaps, an indication of what's at stake here that the facts have so
rarely been examined closely.

Timing

The first problem with the traditional interpretation is timing.
And it is a serious problem. The traditional interpretation has a
simple timeline: On August 6, the U.S. Army Air Forces bomb Hiroshima with a nuclear weapon; three days later, it bombs Nagasaki with another; the next day, the Japanese signal their intention
to surrender.[8] One can hardly blame American newspapers for
running headlines like "Peace in the Pacific: Our Bomb Did It!"[9]

When the story of Hiroshima is told in most American histories, the day of the bombing — August 6 — serves as the narrative
climax. All the elements of the narrative point to that moment: the
decision to build a bomb, the secret research at Los Alamos, the
first impressive test all lead to the final culmination at Hiroshima.
It is told, in other words, as a story about the Bomb. But you can't
objectively analyze Japan's decision to surrender in the context of a
story about the Bomb. Casting it as the story of the Bomb already
presumes that the Bomb's role is central.

Viewed from the Japanese perspective, the most important day
of the war wasn't August 6 but August 9. That was the day that
the Supreme Council met to discuss — for the first time in the war
— unconditional surrender. The Supreme Council was a group of
the top six members of the government — a sort of higher-level
cabinet — who effectively ruled Japan in 1945. Japan's leaders had
not seriously considered surrendering prior to that day. Unconditional surrender (what the Allies were demanding) was a bitter
pill to swallow. The United States and Great Britain were already
convening war-crimes trials in Europe. What if they decided to

put the emperor — who was believed to be divine — on trial? What if the other nations got rid of the emperor and changed Japan's form of government entirely? Even though the situation was bad in the summer of 1945, the leaders of Japan were not willing to contemplate giving up their traditions, their beliefs, or their way of life. Until August 9. What caused them to so suddenly and decisively change their minds? What made them sit down and seriously discuss surrender for the first time after fourteen years of war?

It could not have been Nagasaki. The bombing of Nagasaki occurred in the late morning of the ninth, after the Supreme Council had already begun discussing surrender. Nagasaki can't have been what motivated them to meet.

Hiroshima isn't a very good candidate either. It had come seventy-four hours — more than three days — earlier. What kind of crisis takes three days to unfold? The hallmark of a crisis is a sense of impending disaster and the overwhelming desire to take action *now*. How could Japan's leaders have felt that Hiroshima touched off a crisis and yet not met to talk about the problem for three days?

President John F. Kennedy was sitting up in bed reading the morning papers at about 8:45 A.M. on October 16, 1962, when McGeorge Bundy, his national security adviser, came in to inform him that the Soviet Union was secretly putting nuclear missiles in Cuba. Within two hours and forty-five minutes, a special committee had been created and its members selected, contacted, brought to the White House, and seated around the Cabinet Room table to discuss what should be done.

President Harry Truman was vacationing in Independence, Missouri, on June 24, 1950, when North Korea sent its troops across the 38th Parallel, invading South Korea. Secretary of State Acheson called Truman immediately to give him the news. Within twenty-four hours Truman had flown halfway across the United

States and was seated at Blair House (the White House was undergoing renovations) with his top military and political advisers talking about what to do.

Even Major General George Brinton McClellan, the Union commander of the Army of the Potomac during the Civil War and a man of whom President Lincoln had said sadly, "He's got the *slows*"—even McClellan wasted only twelve hours after he was given a captured copy of General Robert E. Lee's orders for the invasion of Maryland.

These leaders responded—as leaders in any country would—to the imperative call that a crisis creates. They acted decisively, rapidly. How can one square this with the actions of Japan's leaders? If Hiroshima really touched off a crisis that forced the Japanese to surrender after fighting for fourteen years, why did it take them three days to sit down to discuss it?[10]

One might argue that the delay is perfectly logical. Perhaps they came to realize the importance of the bombing only slowly. Perhaps they didn't know it was a nuclear weapon, and when they did realize it and understood the terrible effects such a weapon could have, they naturally concluded they had to surrender. Unfortunately, this explanation doesn't square with the evidence.

Three facts create problems. First, Hiroshima's governor reported to Tokyo on the very day Hiroshima was bombed that about a third of the population had been killed and that two-thirds of the city had been destroyed. This information didn't change over the next several days. So the outcome—the end result of the bombing—was clear from the beginning. Japan's leaders knew roughly what the outcome of the attack was on the first day, yet they still did not act.

Second, the preliminary report on Hiroshima prepared by the Japanese army investigators, the one that gave details about what had happened there, was not delivered until August 10. In other words, it didn't reach Tokyo until *after* the decision to surrender had already been made.[11] Although their verbal report was delivered (to the military) on the eighth, the details of the bombing were not available until two days later. The decision to surrender was therefore not based on a deep appreciation of the horror at Hiroshima.

Third, the Japanese military understood, at least in a general way, what nuclear weapons were. Japan had a nuclear weapons program. Several of the military men mention in their diaries that it was a nuclear weapon that destroyed Hiroshima. General Anami Korechika, minister of war, even went to consult with the head of the Japanese nuclear weapons program on the night of August 7.[12] The idea that Japan's leaders didn't know about nuclear weapons doesn't hold up.[13]

Finally, one other fact about timing creates a striking problem. On August 8, two full days after the bombing of Hiroshima, foreign minister Togo Shigenori went to Premier Suzuki Kantaro and asked that the Supreme Council be convened to discuss the bombing of Hiroshima (the six-member Supreme Council was made up of four military men and two civilians: the army minister, the navy minister, the army chief of staff, the navy chief of staff, the foreign minister, and the prime minister). The fact that a city could be destroyed with a single weapon, Togo presumably argued, was important enough to merit discussion by the council. Suzuki checked with the council members and found that they were unable to make themselves available to meet to discuss the bombing.[14] So the crisis didn't grow day by day until it finally burst into full bloom on August 9. The Supreme Council had considered the need for a meeting about Hiroshima the day before the crucial meeting and decided against it.[15] Any explanation of the actions of Japan's leaders that relies on the shock of the bombing of Hiroshima has to account for the fact that they considered a meeting to discuss the bombing on the eighth, made a judgment that it was too unimportant, and then suddenly decided to meet to discuss surrender the very next day. Either they all succumbed to some sort of group schizophrenia or some other event was the real motivation to discuss surrender.

Based on timing alone, Hiroshima doesn't look like the event that forced Japan's surrender. But there was an event in that second week of August that fits the timing perfectly. At midnight on August 8, the Soviet Union declared war on Japan and began its long-planned invasion of Japan's holdings on the mainland, the southern half of Sakhalin Island, and other territories.[16] Six hours after this news reached Tokyo, the Supreme Council met to discuss unconditional surrender. Clearly the Soviet invasion touched off a crisis, while the bombing of Hiroshima did not.[17]

Scale

From an American perspective it's difficult to imagine that dropping the Bomb wasn't the most important event of the war. The United States had, after all, spent more than two billion dollars (in 1940s dollars) on developing it. Huge facilities were built, and hundreds of top scientists from all across the country were shipped to secret locations in order to work on the project. (There is a story, perhaps apocryphal, that at one point a congressman demanded that a top physicist be brought in to review the Bomb project. He was told it was not possible. Why not? he asked. We can't bring in a top physicist to do an objective review, he was told, because all the top physicists are already working on it.) From the U.S. perspective, the Bomb was clearly important, and it must have seemed natural that it would have an enormous impact.

From the Japanese perspective, however, it might not have been that easy to distinguish the Bomb from other events. It is, after all, difficult to distinguish a single drop of rain in the midst of a rainstorm.

In the summer of 1945, the U.S. Army Air Forces carried out

one of the most intense campaigns of city destruction in the history of the world. Sixty-eight cities in Japan were attacked, and all of them were either partially or completely destroyed. An estimated 1.7 million people were made homeless; 300,000 were killed; and 750,000 were wounded. Sixty-six of these raids were carried out with conventional bombs; two with atomic bombs. The destruction caused by conventional attacks was huge. Night after night, all summer long, cities went up in smoke. In the midst of this cascade of destruction, it would not be surprising if this or that individual attack failed to make much of an impression — even if it was carried out with a remarkable new type of weapon.

A B-29 bomber taking off from the Mariana Islands could carry — depending on the location of the target and the altitude of attack — somewhere between 16,000 and 20,000 pounds of bombs. A typical raid consisted of five hundred bombers. This means that a conventional raid dropped four to five kilotons of bombs on each city.[18] (A kiloton is a thousand tons and is the standard measure of the yield of a nuclear weapon. The Hiroshima bomb measured 16 kilotons; the Nagasaki bomb 20 kilotons.)[19] Given that the use of many bombs spreads the destruction evenly (and therefore more effectively) while a single, more powerful bomb wastes much of its power at the center of the explosion — rebouncing the rubble, as it were — it could be argued that some of the individual conventional raids approached the destruction of the two atomic bombings.

The first of the conventional raids, a night attack on Tokyo on March 9–10, 1945, remains the single most destructive attack on a city in the history of war. Something like sixteen square miles of the city were burned down, roughly the same area as Washington, DC. An estimated one hundred and twenty thousand Japanese lost their lives — the single highest death toll of any bombing attack on any city.[20]

We often imagine, because the horror of it is so often emphasized, that the bombing of Hiroshima was the worst attack on a city in history. We imagine that the number of people killed was off the charts. But if you graph the number of people killed in all the cities bombed in the summer of 1945, you find that Hiroshima was second in terms of civilian deaths.[21] If you chart the number of square miles destroyed, you find that Hiroshima was sixth. If you chart the percentage of the city destroyed, Hiroshima was seventeenth. The attack on Hiroshima was clearly within the parameters of the conventional attacks carried out that summer.[22]

From an American perspective, Hiroshima seems singular, extraordinary. But if you put yourself in the shoes of one of Japan's leaders, the three weeks leading up to the attack on Hiroshima look considerably different. If you were one of the key members of Japan's government in late July and early August, your experience of city bombing would have been something like this: On the morning of July 17, you are greeted by reports that during the night four cities have been attacked—Oita, Hiratsuka, Numazu, and Kuwana. Of these, Oita and Hiratsuka are each more than 50 percent destroyed. Kuwana is more than 75 percent destroyed, and Numazu was hit even more severely, with something like 90 percent of the city burned to the ground.

People killed in each of sixty-eight Japanese cities bombed

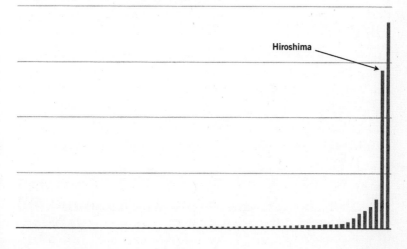

Hiroshima

Three days later, you wake to find that three more cities have been attacked. Fukui is more than 80 percent destroyed. A week later, three more cities are attacked during the night. Two days later, six more cities are attacked in one night, including Ichinomiya, which is 75 percent destroyed. On August 2, you arrive at the office to reports that four more cities have been attacked. And the reports include the information that Toyama (in 1945, roughly the size of Chattanooga, Tennessee) has been 99.5 percent destroyed. Virtually the entire city has been leveled. Four days later, four more cities are attacked. On August 6, only one city, Hiroshima, is attacked, but reports say that the damage is great and a new type of bomb was used. How much does this one new attack stand out against the background of city destruction that has been going on for weeks?

In the three weeks prior to Hiroshima, twenty-six cities were attacked by the U.S. Army Air Forces. Of these, eight—or almost a third—suffered as much or more damage than Hiroshima (in terms of the percentage of the city destroyed). The fact that Japan

Square miles destroyed in each of sixty-eight Japanese cities bombed

had sixty-eight cities devastated in the summer of 1945 poses a serious challenge for people who want to make the bombing of Hiroshima the reason for Japan's surrender. The question is, If the destruction of a city could cause the Japanese to surrender, why didn't they surrender when any of those other sixty-six cities were destroyed?

It is easy to see why Hiroshima might not have stood out much to the Japanese in the parade of destruction that summer.[23] If you look at the following six pictures of city destruction (overleaf), you can see how extensive the bombing damage was. You may also notice that it is difficult to distinguish the nuclear attacks from the conventional attacks. And if you can't readily tell the difference between conventional and nuclear attacks, why would you expect that Japan's leaders could?

Bernard Brodie, dean of nuclear strategists, wrote about the nuclear attacks: "It would be hard to believe that they failed to have a positive and powerful effect on the surrender deliberations, but very little seems to have been said about them in those deliber-

Percent of city destroyed in each of sixty-eight Japanese cities bombed

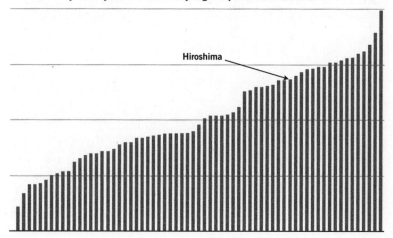

Whole blocks were destroyed.

Some taller buildings survived.

All photos courtesy of the National Archives and Records Administration unless otherwise specified.

Here only isolated buildings still stand.

Traditional Japanese houses were especially vulnerable to fire.

Some cities were left looking like the surface of the moon.

All of these photos depict enormous devastation. However, only the first and second photos (taken at Hiroshima) and the fourth photo (Nagasaki) show the effects of nuclear bombing. The other three photos—taken at Tokyo, Osaka, and again Tokyo, respectively—depict the results of conventional bombing raids.

ations."[24] It would be untrue, however, to say that Japan's leaders didn't make any distinction between the Hiroshima bombing and earlier conventional attacks. They did. They were aware that the explosion had been accompanied by a bright flash of light, which was unusual.[25] They noticed that the destruction was the result of only one or a handful of bombs, since only one or two bombers had been sighted over Hiroshima.[26] The number of casualties was higher than in almost any other bombing, with the important exception of Tokyo's. So there were obviously some differences. But it's not clear that those differences mattered to Japan's leaders very much.

If Japan's leaders surrendered because of Hiroshima and Nagasaki, you would expect to find evidence that they cared about the bombing of cities in general, that the city attacks put pressure on them to surrender. But this doesn't appear to be so. Two days after the bombing of Tokyo, retired foreign minister Shidehara Kijuro expressed a sentiment that was apparently widely held among high-ranking Japanese officials at the time. Shidehara opined that "the people would gradually get used to being bombed daily. In time their unity and resolve would grow stronger." In a letter to a friend he said it was important for citizens to endure the suffering because "even if hundreds of thousands of noncombatants are killed, injured, or starved, even if millions of buildings are destroyed or burned," additional time was needed for diplomacy.[27] It is worth remembering that Shidehara was a moderate.

At the highest levels of government—in the Supreme Council—attitudes were apparently the same. Although the Supreme Council discussed the importance of the Soviet Union remaining neutral, they didn't have a full-dress discussion about the impact of city bombing.[28] In the records of Supreme Council discussions that have been preserved, city bombing is barely *mentioned*. It came up only twice: once in passing in May of 1945, and once during the wide-ranging discussion on the night of August 9.[29] Based on the evidence, it is difficult to make a case that Japan's leaders

thought that city bombing — compared to the other pressing matters involved in running a war — had much significance.

General Anami on August 13 remarked that the atomic bombings were no more menacing than the firebombing that Japan had
endured for months.[30] If the nuclear attacks on Hiroshima and
Nagasaki were no worse than the firebombing attacks on other cities, and if Japan's leaders did not consider city attacks important
enough to discuss in depth, how can the destruction of Hiroshima
and Nagasaki have forced them to surrender?

Reactions

First reactions are often the most telling. Months or years after the
fact, stories tend to change in order to justify, explain, rationalize,
or excuse. What Japan's leaders said and did in the two days after Hiroshima was bombed — before the Soviets entered the war —
provides compelling evidence that they were neither alarmed nor
cowed by the atomic bomb.

Lieutenant General Kawabe Torashiro, for example, wrote in his
diary that he got a "serious jolt" when he realized that an atomic
bomb destroyed Hiroshima. (He uses the word *shigeki,* which is
best translated as "serious jolt," not its cousin *shogeki,* which is
"shock.") It's a peculiar thing that the event that's supposedly going
to force Japan to surrender can't even move the needle of the emotional Richter scale past "serious jolt."[31]

Even more surprising are the next words he wrote in his diary. We must, he said, "be tenacious and fight on." Kawabe does
not sound like a man who is getting ready to surrender the next
day. Of course, Kawabe was one of the most gung-ho members of
Japan's ruling circle, so perhaps it's not surprising that he wasn't
cowed by a nuclear attack.[32] Still, he didn't report that *others* were
worried either.

The diary entry of Admiral Ugaki Matome is similar. He wrote
on August 7: "According to the above, it is clear that this was a ura-

nium atom bomb and it deserves to be regarded as a real wonder, making the outcome of the war more gloomy. We must think of some countermeasures against it immediately, and at the same time I wish we could create the same bomb."[33] Ugaki's reaction was a mix of admiration and jealousy. He wished Japan could build a bomb. And his emotions seemed surprisingly mild. His judgment was that it made the outcome "more gloomy." He did not say, for example, *Now we are forced to surrender.*

Most convincing of all was a conversation on August 8 between Admiral Yonai Mitsumasa and Admiral Takagi Sokichi, recorded in Takagi's diary.[34] It is too long to reproduce here, but it is a remarkable window into the state of mind of two of Japan's most highly placed officials. (Yonai, remember, was on the Supreme Council.) Reading the conversation leaves one with the impression that these men felt no real sense of crisis. Yonai and Takagi talk like men in the midst of difficulty, but clearly they believe there is still time to act. In fact, Takagi even says the government shouldn't get too complacent about how long it would be before U.S. forces invade. The "real problem" facing Japan, Takagi says, was declining enthusiasm for the war among ordinary people. The notion that the real problem facing Japan was bombardment by a new type of bomb didn't seem to cross his mind.

And the way in which the Bomb was mentioned in this conversation—entirely in passing—is peculiar. How can the Bomb not be the center of their whole talk? Takagi mentions the Bomb, and Yonai responds by bringing up rice rationing. It isn't a stretch to think that Yonai believed that rice rationing (and the possibility that hunger could trigger a popular uprising) was a more serious problem than the bombing of Hiroshima.

It is remarkable to read the way these men talked. They are sizing up who's influential, who is likely to be with them in the debate about resolving the war as quickly as possible, who should talk to whom, what the Soviet leader Joseph Stalin might do and when, and what steps should be taken next. They're being facetious and making jokes at the expense of Premier Suzuki. They are *not* saying: *Everything is over. Now we'll have to surrender.* Whatever event was going to force that decision on them, it had yet to occur.[35]

While reactions to the bombing of Hiroshima seemed strangely subdued, the reactions of Japan's leaders to the Soviet entry into the war were strikingly different. When cabinet secretary Sakomizu Hisatsune was awoken in the early-morning hours of August 9 and told that the Soviets had invaded Manchuria, he was overwhelmed with rage, "as if all the blood in my body flowed backward."[36] He remembered the time and place and *exactly* how it felt. He was flooded with emotion. The emotional blankness of the postwar accounts of the impact of Hiroshima are remarkable by comparison.

And more telling than what they said is what they did. On the morning that the Soviets invaded Manchuria, orders were drawn up declaring martial law in Japan and preparations for implementing them were begun.[37] No such orders had been put in place three days earlier when Hiroshima was bombed. On the morning that the Soviets attacked, deputy chief of staff of the army Kawabe, in the army-only meeting that was held to discuss what should be done, raised the possibility of setting up a military dictatorship.[38] No such emergency meeting was held and no such drastic measures were discussed after the bombing of Hiroshima. The Supreme Council didn't meet to discuss the bombing of Hiroshima, yet they were seated at the table discussing surrender within six hours of learning that the Soviets had declared war.[39] Based on the things officials said and the actions they took, it seems clear that the Soviet declaration of war touched off a crisis while the bombing of Hiroshima did not.

Strategic Significance

If the Japanese were not concerned with city bombing in general or the atomic bombing of Hiroshima in particular, what were they concerned with? The answer is simple: the Soviet Union. In the summer of 1945, all eyes in Japan were turned toward Moscow.

The Japanese were in a relatively difficult strategic situation. They were nearing the end of a war they were losing badly. Conditions continued to deteriorate. The army, however, was still strong and well supplied. Nearly 4 million men were under arms, and 1.2 million of them were guarding Japan's home islands.

Even the most hard-line leaders in Japan's government knew that the war could not go on. The question was not whether to continue, but how to bring the war to a close under the best terms possible. The Allies (the United States, Great Britain, and others — the Soviet Union, remember, was still neutral at that point) were demanding unconditional surrender. Japan's leaders hoped to figure out a way to avoid war-crimes trials; they also wanted to preserve their form of government, and they wanted to keep some of the territories they'd conquered: Korea, Vietnam, Burma, parts of Malaysia and Indonesia, a large portion of eastern China, and numerous islands in the Pacific.

They had two different plans for getting better surrender terms; in other words, they had two strategic options. The first was diplomatic. Japan had signed a five-year neutrality pact with the Soviets in April of 1941 that would expire in 1946. A group consisting mostly of civilian leaders and led by foreign minister Togo Shigenori hoped that Stalin might be convinced to mediate a settlement between the United States and its allies on the one hand and Japan on the other. Even though this plan was a long shot, it reflected sound strategic thinking. After all, it would be in the interests of the Soviet Union to make sure that the terms of the settlement were not too favorable to the United States; any increase in U.S. influence and power in Asia would mean a decrease in Russian power and influence.

The second plan was military, and most of its proponents, led by the army minister Anami Korechika, were military men. They hoped to use imperial army ground troops to inflict high casualties on U.S. forces when those forces invaded. If they succeeded, the military men felt, they might be able to get the United States to offer better terms. This strategy was also a long shot. The United States seemed deeply committed to unconditional surrender. But since there was, in fact, concern in U.S. military circles that the casualties in an invasion would be prohibitively high, the Japanese command's strategy was not entirely off the mark.[40]

One way to determine whether it was the bombing of Hiroshima or the invasion and declaration of war by the Soviet Union that caused Japan's surrender is to compare the ways in which these two events affected the strategic situation. After Hiroshima was bombed on August 8, both options were still alive. It would still have been possible to ask Stalin to mediate (and Takagi's diary entries from the eighth of August show that at least some of Japan's leaders were still thinking about the effort to get Stalin involved). It would also still have been possible to try to fight one last decisive battle and inflict heavy casualties. The destruction of Hiroshima had done nothing to reduce the preparedness of the troops on the beaches of Japan's home islands. There was now one fewer city behind them, but they were still dug in, they still had ammunition, and their military strength had not been diminished in any important way. The bombing of Hiroshima did not foreclose either of Japan's strategic options.

The impact of the Soviet declaration of war and invasion of Manchuria and Sakhalin Island was quite different, however. Once the Soviet Union declared war, Stalin could no longer act as a mediator — he was now a belligerent. So the diplomatic option was wiped out by the Soviet move. The effect on the military situation was equally dramatic. Most of Japan's best troops had been shifted to the southern part of the home islands. Japan's military had correctly guessed that the likely first target of an American invasion would be the southernmost island of Kyushu, so they had gradually shifted forces to Kyushu. The once proud Kwangtung army in

Manchuria was a shell of its former self because its best units had been stripped away to defend Japan proper. When the Russians invaded Manchuria, they sliced through what had once been an elite army, and many Russian units stopped only when they ran out of gas. The Soviet Sixteenth Army—a hundred thousand strong—launched an invasion of the southern half of Sakhalin Island. Their orders were to mop up Japanese resistance there, and then—within ten to fourteen days—be prepared to invade Hokkaido, the northernmost of Japan's home islands. The Japanese force tasked with defending Hokkaido, the Fifth Area Army, was understrength at two divisions and two brigades, and it was in fortified positions on the *east* side of the island. The Soviet plan of attack called for an invasion of Hokkaido from the *west*.

It didn't take a military genius to see that, although it might have been possible to fight a decisive battle against one great power invading from one direction, it was not possible to fight off two great powers attacking from two different directions. The Soviet invasion precluded the military's decisive-battle strategy, just as it precluded the diplomatic strategy. At a single stroke, all of Japan's options evaporated. The Soviet entry into the war was strategically decisive (it foreclosed both of Japan's options), while the bombing of Hiroshima (which foreclosed neither) was not.

The Soviet declaration of war also changed the Japanese calculation of how much time was left to maneuver. Japanese intelligence had predicted that U.S. forces might not invade for months. Soviet forces, on the other hand, could be in Japan proper in as little as ten days. The Soviet invasion made Japan's decision on ending the war extremely time sensitive. From the Japanese perspective, the Soviet intervention was decisive.

And Japan's leaders had already reached this conclusion. In a meeting of the Supreme Council in June of 1945, they said that Soviet entry into the war "would determine the fate of the Empire." Army deputy chief of staff Kawabe said in that same meeting that "the absolute maintenance of peace in our relations with the Soviet Union is imperative for the continuation of the war."[41]

Japan's leaders consistently displayed a lack of interest in the bombing that was wrecking their cities. And while this might have been wrong when the bombing began in March of 1945, by the time Hiroshima was hit, they were certainly right to see protecting their cities as a barn door that was no longer worth closing: that horse had run off long ago. When Truman famously threatened to visit a "rain of ruin" on Japanese cities if Japan did not surrender, few people in the United States realized that there was little left to destroy. By August 7, only ten cities larger than a hundred thousand people had not already been bombed.[42] Nagasaki was attacked on August 9, and that left nine. Three of those were on the northernmost island of Hokkaido and were therefore out of range of attacks from Tinian Island, where American planes were based.[43] Kyoto, the ancient capital of Japan, had been removed from the target list by Secretary of War Henry Stimson because of its religious and symbolic importance. So, despite the fearsome sound of Truman's threat, after Nagasaki was bombed, only five major cities remained that could readily be hit with atomic weapons.

Of course, it would have been possible to re-bomb cities that had already been attacked with conventional bombs. But these cities were, on average, already 50 percent destroyed. Or the United States could have bombed smaller cities with atomic weapons. The U.S. Army Air Forces campaign had been so tenaciously thorough, however, that only six smaller cities (those with populations between 30,000 and 100,000) remained that had not already been bombed. And three of them were out of range.[44] Given that Japan had already had major bombing damage done to sixty-eight cities and had, for the most part, shrugged it off, it is perhaps not surprising that Japan's leaders were unimpressed with the threat of further bombing. It was not strategically compelling.

Proponents of nuclear weapons who claim that Japan was

forced to surrender because of the bombing of Hiroshima face a difficult question: Why would Japan's leaders have been motivated to act by an event that was *not* strategically decisive? And if—as proponents of the Hiroshima-as-cause-of-surrender must argue—Japan's leaders ignored the Soviet entry into the war, an event that *was* strategically decisive, what were they thinking?

In order for the traditional interpretation of Hiroshima to be true, it is necessary to believe that Japan's leaders did not know their business. Their job was to understand what mattered to Japan and to base their decisions on the strategic factors that would affect the outcome of the war and the long-term health and safety of Japan. Their job was not to be emotionally appalled by horrific acts or to be swayed by feelings of pity toward civilians or by any other sorts of feelings; their job was to weigh the strategic factors in Japan's situation and respond accordingly.[45] Hiroshima was not decisive. The Soviet declaration of war and imminent invasion was. How could Japan's leaders have taken the first seriously and ignored the second?

An Emotionally Convenient Story

Ideas can persist because they are true, but unfortunately, they can also persist because they are emotionally satisfying: they fill important psychic needs. Despite the existence of these four powerful objections, the traditional interpretation retains a strong hold on many people's thinking, particularly in the United States. There is real resistance to looking at the facts. But perhaps this should not be surprising. It is worth reminding ourselves how emotionally convenient the traditional explanation of Hiroshima is—for both Japan and the United States. For example, at the end of the war, the traditional interpretation of Hiroshima helped Japan's leaders achieve a number of important political aims, both domestic and international.

Put yourself in the shoes of the emperor. You have just led

your country through a disastrous war. The economy is shattered. Eighty percent of your cities have been bombed and burned. The army has been pummeled and suffered a string of defeats. The navy has been decimated and is confined to port. Starvation is looming. The war, in short, has been a catastrophe, and, worse, you've been lying to your people about how bad the situation really is. They will be shocked by news of surrender. So do you admit that you failed badly? Issue a statement saying that you miscalculated, made repeated mistakes, and did enormous damage to the nation? Or would you rather blame the loss on an amazing scientific breakthrough that no one could have predicted? In a single stroke, blaming the loss of the war on the atomic bomb swept all mistakes and misjudgments under the rug. The Bomb was the perfect explanation for having lost the war. No need to apportion blame; no need to hold a court of inquiry. Japan's leaders could claim they had done their best.[46] So at the most general level, the Bomb served to deflect blame from Japan's leaders.

But attributing Japan's defeat to the Bomb also served three other specific political purposes. First, it helped to preserve the legitimacy of the emperor. If the war was lost not because of mistakes but because of the enemy's unexpected miracle weapon, then the institution of the emperor might continue to find support within Japan.

Second, it appealed to international sympathy. Japan had waged war aggressively and with particular brutality toward conquered peoples. Their behavior was likely to be condemned by other nations. Japan's being able to recast itself as a victimized nation — one that had been unfairly bombed with a cruel and horrifying instrument of war — would help offset some of the morally repugnant things Japan's military had done. Drawing attention to the atomic bombings painted Japan in a more sympathetic light and deflected demands for harsh punishment.

Finally, Japan's saying that the Bomb had won the war would

please Japan's American victors. The American occupation of Japan did not officially end until 1952, and during that time the United States had the power to change or remake Japanese society as it saw fit. In the early days of the occupation, many Japanese officials worried that the Americans intended to abolish the institution of the emperor. And they had another worry. Many of Japan's top government officials knew that they might be tried for war crimes (the war-crimes trials against Germany's leaders were already under way when Japan surrendered). Japanese historian Asada Sadao has said that in many of the postwar interviews, "Japanese officials . . . were obviously anxious to please their American questioners."[47] If the Americans wanted to believe that the Bomb won the war, why not let them?

So attributing the end of the war to the atomic bomb served Japan's interests in multiple ways. But it also served U.S. interests. If the Bomb won the war, then the perception of U.S. military power would be enhanced; U.S. diplomatic influence in Asia and around the world would increase; and U.S. security would be strengthened. The two billion dollars spent on the Bomb would not have been wasted. But if the Soviet entry into the war was what had caused Japan to surrender, then the Soviets could claim that they had been able to do in four days what the United States was unable to do in four years, and the perception of Soviet military power and Soviet diplomatic influence would be enhanced. It is easy to see how Japan's attributing the U.S. victory to the Bomb might flatter American pride as well as serve U.S. interests. And denying that the actions of the Soviet Union had influenced Japan's decision to surrender would soon become a matter of patriotism for Americans: Once the Cold War was under way, asserting that the Soviet entry into the war had been the decisive factor would be tantamount to giving aid and comfort to the enemy. It is not surprising that few people in the United States made that suggestion in the 1950s and 1960s.[48]

One reason that it is so difficult to see the surrender of Japan clearly is that there is so much at stake for everyone concerned. Emotional needs are challenged. Considerations of national pride come into play. Myths bathe us in a warm, mellow light that shows off our best features and hides our flaws. Myths make us comfortable. Facts throw off only a harsh, disinterested light. But when an issue as dangerous as nuclear war is our concern, it would be foolish to choose a pleasing fiction over an ugly reality.

The Cover-Up

So are we to believe that the emperor and all the top officials of his government were lying? That there was a grand conspiracy to mislead the world about why Japan surrendered?

As a general rule, wide-ranging conspiracies are difficult because it's so hard to keep everyone on message. As Benjamin Franklin said, "Three may keep a secret, if two of them are dead." But in this case, the highly conformist nature of Japanese society and the strong motive to preserve the legitimacy of the Meiji regime may have compensated to some extent for the difficulty of maintaining unity. The eagerness of Americans to believe that "our bomb won it" may also have helped perpetuate the story.

Over the past twenty years, scholars have increasingly raised questions about the reliability of the postwar accounts of the participants. For example, Japanese historian Hatano Sumio says that few of the statements, memoirs, and biographies by top leaders "contain reliable accounts." Herbert Bix, author of a Pulitzer Prize–winning biography of the emperor, argues that postwar accounts were considerably altered to protect the emperor and obscure his participation in wartime decisions.[49] Historian Richard Frank agreed, throwing doubt on parts of the account of Kido Koichi.[50]

And a careful examination of the record confirms the suspicion of a cover-up. Navy Minister Yonai was a staunch supporter of immediate surrender and one of the few military men who was concerned that civilian unrest would lead to open revolt. Here he talks with his subordinate Admiral Takagi on August 12, 1945, after surrender has been offered but not yet agreed to.

> I think the term is inappropriate, but the atomic bombs and the Soviet entry into the war are, in a sense, gifts from the gods [*tenyu*, also "Heaven-sent blessings"]. This way we don't have to say that we have quit the war because of domestic circumstances. Why I have long been advocating control of the crisis of the country is neither from fear of an enemy attack nor because of the atomic bombs and the Soviet entry into the war. The main reason is my anxiety over the domestic situation. So, it is rather fortunate that now we can control matters without revealing the domestic situation.[51]

What is striking here is Yonai's matter-of-fact presumption that Japan's leaders would conceal the real reasons why they surrendered. His relief is palpable — the ability to put the blame for defeat on something other than the real reason is a "gift from the gods." Even if Yonai's analysis of why it was vital for Japan to surrender is a minority opinion, his attitude stands as a clear warning that we should not take the Japanese leaders' stated reasons for surrender at face value.

Yonai's statement is indirect evidence. Kido Koichi's statement is much more forthright. Kido was privy seal and one of the advisers closest to the emperor. He said after the war that the Bomb played a role in persuading the military to accept surrender, not because of its strategic importance but rather because of the emotional role it played. "If military leaders could convince themselves that they were defeated by the power of science but not by lack of spiritual power or strategic errors, they could save face to some extent."[52] Secretary of the cabinet Sakomizu Hisatsune, who was, according to historian Herbert Bix, one of a key group of younger officials who worked behind the scenes to manage the surrender, explained in his postwar interview with U.S. interrogators:

The chance had come to end the war. It was not necessary to blame the military side, the manufacturing people, or anyone else — just the atomic bomb. It was a good excuse, someone said that the atomic bomb was the Kamikaze [the divine wind that miraculously destroyed the invading Mongol fleet in 1281] to save Japan.[53]

In a later publication called "The Truth About Surrender" he was even more explicit.

The atomic bomb was a golden opportunity given by Heaven for Japan to end the war. There were those who said that the Japanese armed forces were not defeated. It was in science that Japan was defeated, so the military will not bring shame on themselves by surrendering. . . . In ending the war, the idea was to put the responsibility for defeat solely on the atomic bomb, not on the military. This was a clever pretext.[54]

It is startling to hear one of the key players describe the atomic bombing not as the powerful event that forced surrender but as an incident used as a clever pretext to save face for the military.[55] How can anyone take the argument that the Bomb forced surrender seriously when several key actors say that the Bomb story was merely a cover-up to win sympathy from the people and salve the military's shame?

Conclusion

It is troubling to consider, given the questions raised here, that the evidence of Hiroshima and Nagasaki is at the heart of everything most people think they know about nuclear weapons. This event is the bedrock of the case for the importance of nuclear weapons. It is crucial to their unique status, to the notion that the normal rules do not apply to these weapons. It is an important measure of nuclear threats: Truman's threat to visit a "rain of ruin" on Japan was the first explicit nuclear threat. It is key to the "aura" of enormous power that surrounds the weapons and makes them so important in international relations.

But what are we to make of all those conclusions if the traditional story of Hiroshima is called into doubt? Hiroshima is the center, the point from which all other claims and assertions radiate out. Yet the traditional story does not seem well connected to the facts. What are we to think about nuclear weapons if this enormous first accomplishment — the miracle of Japan's sudden surrender — turns out to be a myth?

Myth 2

H-BOMB QUANTUM LEAP

I N 1952 A NEW TYPE of nuclear weapon was tested by the United States. The H-bomb used hydrogen along with uranium and was, it was said, "thousands of times" bigger than the bomb that had devastated Hiroshima. Most people found it difficult to imagine a bomb that was a thousand times bigger than the Hiroshima bomb. But it was not hard to imagine that such a bomb represented a quantum leap in the power of nuclear weapons. The conclusion that most people drew was that the new bombs must be decisive in war.

The notion that the decade of the 1950s was a time of decisive change in nuclear weaponry is now a commonplace in histories of nuclear weapons, a conclusion that can be relied upon as fact. But it turns out that the revolution introduced by the H-bomb was more illusion than reality. There are sound reasons for wondering if the lesson the public learned from this episode — that the bombs were surely decisive in war — is true.

H-Bomb Revolution

The H-bomb was epochal. McGeorge Bundy, who served as President Kennedy's national security adviser, said the decision to de-

velop the H-bomb was "the second great step of the nuclear age."[1]
British prime minister Winston Churchill said of the H-bomb:

> There is an immense gulf between the atomic bomb and the hy-
> drogen bomb. The atomic bomb, with all its terrors, did not carry
> us outside the scope of human control or manageable events, in
> thought or action, in peace or war . . . [but with the advent] of the
> hydrogen bomb, the entire foundation of human affairs was rev-
> olutionized, and mankind placed in a situation both measureless
> and laden with doom.[2]

One reason people were so impressed with the H-bomb is
that the way the size of nuclear weapons is measured — by something called yield — is misleading. The yield of a nuclear bomb is
defined as the weight of conventional weaponry — TNT — that
would be needed to make an equivalent explosion. Yield exagger-
ates the difference in size between weapons, particularly as the size
of the weapon gets larger. It's a funny measure, in any case, when
you stop and think about it. It's a little like calculating the power
that a car engine generates in terms of the *weight* of the number of
horses that would be needed to produce an equivalent pull. We're
interested in how destructive nuclear weapons are. Why not develop a standard of measurement that expresses a bomb's power in
terms of the area a bomb would destroy?

As lay people, we imagine that when someone describes the
size of a bomb, he is describing the size of the destruction it will
produce. We imagine, in other words, that there is a one-to-one
equivalence between yield and destructiveness, between the size of
the bomb and the area it destroys. But yield doesn't actually give
a very accurate picture of this. Consider the difference between
the Hiroshima bomb, whose yield is estimated at fifteen kilotons,
and a one-megaton nuclear bomb. Yield is about weight, so it is
measured in kilotons (thousands of tons) and megatons (millions
of tons). A one-megaton bomb makes an explosion the equiva-

lent of one million tons of TNT. In terms of yield, a one-megaton bomb is 66.7 times bigger than the bomb dropped on Hiroshima, which might lead you to expect it would be 66.7 times more destructive. When I first read about the difference in the sizes of nuclear explosions, I thought of the kind of map that is common in books about nuclear weapons: an aerial view of the city with concentric rings drawn on it to show the different zones of destruction. When I tried to envision the difference in scale between a one-megaton bomb and the Hiroshima bomb, I imagined the radii of those rings multiplied by 66.7. But this illustrates why yield is misleading. The radius of the innermost circle of a one-megaton bomb isn't 66.7 times greater than the radius of the innermost circle of the Hiroshima bomb; it's 5.5 times greater.[3] Calculating the destruction that various sizes of bombs would create is complicated, and yield does a particularly poor job of representing the differences.[4]

Hydrogen bombs are fearsome weapons. They are enormously destructive. Any war fought with them would be a disaster. But although they are "thousands of times" bigger in terms of yield, they are not "thousands of times" bigger in terms of destruction.

There is another problem with the lessons learned from the H-bomb revolution. Over the past forty years, a curious thing has been happening to the sizes of explosions that bombs are designed to produce: they've been getting smaller. There is no theoretical limit to the size of hydrogen bombs. You could conceivably add more and more hydrogen to the bomb and increase the size of the explosion forever. Infinitely large bombs are imaginable. But bombs have not been getting bigger; they've been getting smaller. In the late 1950s and early 1960s, bombs measuring nine megatons were common in the U.S. and Soviet arsenals. But over time, war planners called for smaller and smaller weapons. Today, the average yield of the weapons in the U.S. arsenal is something like 175 kilotons.[5] That's only about ten times bigger than the Hiroshima bomb in terms of yield. The destructiveness of nuclear weapons today is not all that much greater than that of the bombs used to destroy Hiroshima and Nagasaki. It certainly isn't thousands of times bigger.

So the first thing to know about the H-bomb revolution is that, as a technical matter having to do with the size of the bombs, it doesn't exist. There may have been some sort of limited revolution in the 1950s, but there is certainly nothing like it today.

Strategic Bombing Is Decisive?

What nuclear strategists learned from the events of the 1950s was that strategic bombing is decisive. Strategic bombing — attacking the cities, industries, and military installations located in your enemy's homeland — is a task that nuclear weapons are ideally suited for. But there are reasons to question whether this assumption of nuclear thinking is true.

By the 1950s, according to historian Lawrence Freedman, the decisiveness of strategic bombing was an accepted fact.[6] There had been doubts about strategic bombing in World War II. Enormous resources had been devoted to bombing Germany and Japan, and many other countries had had their cities bombed, but there was no clear consensus on whether the bombing had worked. Conventional bombing by itself had not forced either Germany or Japan to surrender. And the bombing campaigns had been enormously expensive in effort, money, and lives. The debate was so sharp and the divisions so deep that the United States commissioned the U.S. Strategic Bombing Survey (USSBS), a massive, multivolume study of the effectiveness of strategic bombing. The USSBS is extraordinary for the breadth and depth of its coverage of the bombing in World War II. Its conclusion: strategic bombing helped but was not decisive.

Most of the nuclear strategists agreed. Bernard Brodie wrote, "The Allies learned after the war that the attack on enemy morale had been on the whole a waste of bombs. . . . In World War II the effects of bombing on civilian morale were certainly not trivial, but it seems clear that the lowered morale resulting from bombing did not importantly affect military operations or the outcome of the war."[7] Thomas Schelling wrote, "Blockade and strategic bombing by themselves were not quite up to the job in either world war in Europe. . . . Airplanes could not quite make punitive, coercive violence decisive in Europe."[8]

But by the 1950s, all that had changed. Almost all the strategists in the United States agreed that, while strategic bombing had not been decisive in World War II, it was certainly decisive now. No serious student of nuclear weapons raised the possibility that strategic bombing with nuclear weapons could fail. It was a remarkable turn of events. Strategists were unsure of the efficacy of a particular kind of military attack, and then, in a very short time, they became certain it could not fail. It is worth asking what changed their minds. What new evidence emerged between the time when the U.S. Strategic Bombing Survey was commissioned, in 1944, and the early years of the 1950s? The answer is simple: Hiroshima and Nagasaki. The evidence that changed people's minds about strategic bombing was the surprising, unexpected, and complete victory that apparently resulted from bombing Hiroshima and Nagasaki with nuclear weapons.[9]

It is disconcerting, given the review of facts in the previous chapter and the considerable doubts that that review raises, to realize that this is used as the main piece of evidence that strategic bombing really works. Before Hiroshima, they weren't sure; after Hiroshima, they were sure. Except we now know that there are reasons to doubt the lesson that was learned from Hiroshima. If we were wrong about Hiroshima and Nagasaki, could we be wrong about strategic bombing too?

Destroying Cities

One way to gain perspective on the efficacy of attacking cities with nuclear weapons is to look at examples from the past. There is clear historical evidence — present throughout all ages — that city attacks do not coerce. Review the most famous wars of history — World War II, World War I, the Napoleonic wars, and so on — and there is little evidence that any of them was won by attacks on cities or civilians. Even if one turns to lesser-known but far more extreme cases where attacks against cities and civilians were egregious, there is little support for the idea that destroying cities or killing civilians wins wars. Genghis Khan, for example, during his campaign in the central Asian empire of Khwarazm from 1219 to 1221, infamously made a practice of destroying cities and slaughtering their inhabitants. Bokhara, Merv, Samarkand, and Urganch were among the cities he destroyed. Despite the campaign's ferocity, cities were still offering resistance three years after the start of the war. If the threat of city destruction delivers reliable leverage, all the cities of the Khwarazmian Empire would have surrendered after the first few cities were destroyed. But cities continued to resist until the last Khwarazmian army was defeated, on the banks of the Indus in 1221. In 1631, during the Thirty Years' War, the city of Magdeburg was burned and most of its citizens slaughtered. If city destruction were an important military event, the war would have ended soon after that. In fact, the war went on for seventeen more years. In 1943, British and American air forces devastated the city of Hamburg. But Germany did not surrender for two more years.

There is a long history of armies destroying cities in war. There are almost no instances, however, of a country giving up because one of its cities was destroyed. This is in keeping with the American experience of war as well. In the fall of 1864, the Union general William T. Sherman captured the city of Atlanta, then the twelfth-largest city in the South. Sherman, who had said, "I would make this war as severe as possible, and show no symptoms of tiring till the South begs for mercy," burned Atlanta to the ground. But the South fought on.

In April of 1865, after years of fruitless effort, Northern armies finally captured the Rebel capital of Richmond, Virginia. Richmond had long been the holy grail of the North's war effort. Numerous commentators and even popular songs ("On to Richmond!") voiced the sentiment that if the Rebel capital could be captured, the rebellion itself would collapse. In the event, however, Southerners fought stubbornly on.

The South did not surrender when Atlanta was burned or Richmond was captured. Defeat occurred only when the *armies* of Generals Lee and Johnston were forced to surrender. The destruction of Atlanta and the capture of Richmond were incidental to the war effort, not central.

The question is not whether nuclear weapons can physically destroy cities in a matter of hours. The physics of nuclear explosions are well known and beyond doubt. The question is what people would do in response. Would they give up? The evidence from history contradicts the intuition that they would surrender. Destroying cities has never led to surrender.

Of course, a nuclear war would be different. The attacks against cities wouldn't occur one by one; they would occur all at once. And perhaps that would make a difference. But it is important to admit that no one knows. We are all speculating. It seems logical that the destruction of a large number of cities would make people in that country feel helpless, but the evidence contradicts this logic.

Using History

One response to the evidence about destroying cities is to argue, as Kevin Drum has, that "it's not World War II anymore." Drum is absolutely right: it's not World War II anymore. But "times have changed" isn't a persuasive argument for dismissing the evidence of the past. Things are always different. By that logic, you could argue that the sun won't come up today because "it's not yesterday anymore." Lessons from the past often apply even when the technology in our lives has changed. This is why, even though we have flat-screen TVs and cell phones, people still fall in love, they still dance, they still fight wars, and most prestigious universities still have departments of history. We study the past and use it as a guide because doing so often predicts how humans will behave in the future. When faced with a difficult problem, most people would gladly trade a bucketful of theorizing for even a thimbleful of real experience.

At its heart, Drum's argument is the nuclear-exceptionalism argument, which asserts that nuclear weapons are so different that the rules from the past no longer apply. This is the same point that most nuclear strategists made in the 1950s. Herman Kahn aptly summed up the conventional wisdom among nuclear strategists when he wrote:

> Despite the fact that nuclear weapons have already been used twice, and the nuclear sword has been rattled many times, one can argue that for all practical purposes nuclear war is still (and hopefully will remain) so far from our experience that it is difficult to reason from, or illustrate arguments by, analogies from history. Thus, many of our concepts and doctrines must be based on abstract and analytical considerations.[10]

The lessons of the past would still apply to a nuclear war, however, because even though nuclear weapons are new, human beings are largely the same. Even if the tools are different, the people using them have not fundamentally changed their nature. War has a relatively strong continuity across history because it is fought by people. And the character of human beings changes only very slowly, if at all. The ancient Greek playwright Euripides wrote movingly about the cruelty of slavery in 424 B.C.[11] Two thousand years later most nations have formally outlawed slavery, which is progress, but there are still large numbers of children and women who live in conditions that quite closely resemble the slavery of ancient Greece. Sex slaves and child soldiers are held captive and forced to do things against their will in ways that ancient Greek slaves would have found entirely familiar.

The past was different. Our ancestors wore different clothes and used different everyday implements. They organized their lives and societies differently. But even though the externals are different, some core elements remain the same. The names and habits of people in the Bible are sometimes strange, but we recognize the seven deadly sins with ease.

I am not arguing that people never change. The ancient Greeks, for example, had no concept corresponding to the modern idea of the unconscious. The notion of a conscious, rational mind really began to emerge only in the fifth century B.C.[12] Human ideas and conceptions evolve. Yet we can read ancient Greek tragedy and feel the power of the deeply human emotions they evoke. Evolution is slow, not fast. Changes in fundamental human traits and attitudes take hundreds or thousands of years. We can change our clothes, but it is much, much harder to change our hearts.

The fact that a nuclear war would be fought with new tools does not substantially change our behavior or our reactions to war. Dismissing the lessons of the past because nuclear weapons are new is to risk falling into the trap that Santayana warned about: "Those who cannot remember the past are condemned to repeat it."

Destruction

Embedded in the belief that strategic bombing must be decisive is an assumption that destroying things will advance one's cause in war. People often talk about nuclear weapons' ability to create destruction as if it were an accepted fact that destruction and military effectiveness are the same thing. But although wars are often accompanied by destruction, that is not what they are about.

Destruction does not win wars. Consider Stalingrad, a city at the bend of the Volga River that was the high-water mark of the German efforts to conquer Russia during World War II. In the fall of 1942, the Germans destroyed much of the city with bombing and artillery. They killed or drove away almost all of Stalingrad's citizens. Yet they did not win the battle of Stalingrad, because they did not defeat the Soviet soldiers that clung tenaciously to its ruins. War is about soldiers. Destroying cities and killing civilians is largely beside the point in terms of military strategy.

There is a great deal of destruction in war, and sometimes the loser in war suffers more destruction than the winner. But that does not prove a connection between how much destruction occurs and who wins. Consider the war between France and Russia in 1812. The invasion of Russia launched by Napoleon in June of that year is justly considered the turning point in the Napoleonic wars. The French army of 690,000 men was the largest force ever assembled in a European war up to that point. All of the fighting took place on Russian soil, and most of the battles were either French victories or draws. The destruction suffered in Russia during this campaign was extraordinary. As they advanced deeper and deeper into Russia, the huge French army left a swath of ravaged crops and livestock, burned villages, and other kinds of economic and social destruction.

The destruction was crowned by the burning of Moscow, not then the capital of Russia but perhaps the spiritual center of the realm. As Napoleon's armies won victory after victory, and particularly after the battle of Borodino, it became clear to the Russian authorities that Moscow was likely to fall. They determined to strip the city of all food, supplies, and any items that could be used by the French. The population was evacuated; useful items were removed or destroyed; and the city was abandoned. The French found an empty city with almost nothing worth having in it. What happened next is still a matter of dispute. Some say the French burned Moscow in disgust. Some say the Russians themselves lit the city on fire as they left as part of a scorched-earth policy. At any rate, the city burned, and by the time the fires subsided, four-fifths of Moscow had been turned to ashes. What had once been a thriving metropolis was now a blackened ruin sending wisps of smoke across the steppes.

Russia suffered far more destruction during this war than France did. No armies crisscrossed France, pillaging and plundering. No French cities were burned. (Russia's allies, including Great Britain, carried out operations against the French fleet, French possessions overseas, and French shore installations, but this damage was trivial in the overall scope of the war.) For all intents and purposes, all of the destruction occurred in Russia. Yet the French lost. The key to the Russian campaign was what happened to Napoleon's *army,* not to Russia's civilians, cities, or economy. By the time Napoleon returned from Russia, casualties and attrition from the long and frightful retreat through the brutal Russian winter had wiped out roughly 90 percent of the Grande Armée that had marched so proudly into Russia six months earlier.[13]

Destruction does not determine who wins or loses a war. It is possible for one side to suffer enormous destruction and yet still win. Destroying your opponent's economic resources and especially his military industries can help. But it is not clear how much it helps. How much destruction is necessary before the damage becomes decisive? Japan had sixty-eight cities (and the industries in them) destroyed without its surrendering. Winning and losing wars depends on whether your adversary's military is defeated, not how much damage is done to its civilians and their houses, businesses, and country. People who write about nuclear weapons often confuse general destruction with destruction that directly contributes to the defeat of an adversary's military. Destroying is not the same as winning.

Conclusion

The lesson people learned from advances in nuclear weapons technology in the 1950s was that nuclear war was decisive. Such massive explosions surely had to be decisive. There's no question that they were partly right: nuclear weapons are enormously destructive, and any war in which a lot of nuclear weapons are used would be a catastrophe. But it's not clear that nuclear weapons are necessarily decisive or even particularly useful weapons of war. The increase in size of nuclear weapons was exaggerated and has largely been offset by reductions in the sizes of warheads since. The H-bomb revolution may have had an effect in the 1950s, but it has little effect today. It's not clear that causing all that destruction and killing all those civilians necessarily brings victory. Nuclear weapons are enormously dangerous. Looking closely at nuclear war is uncomfortable, but that is no excuse for imprecision. Loose thinking and slipshod judgments will not yield sensible policy.

NUCLEAR DETERRENCE WORKS IN A CRISIS

N UCLEAR DETERRENCE WORKS. It works robustly. It works reliably. And most of all, it works in a crisis. At least, those are the assumptions that exist in many people's minds, particularly those people now in their fifties and sixties. The experience of living through a series of crises during the Cold War strongly influenced their ideas about nuclear deterrence. In the early 1950s, nuclear deterrence was just a theory, just some notion that strategists in think tanks like RAND had imagined. But by the end of the 1960s most people were sure that nuclear deterrence really worked. They'd lived through these crises, after all, and *something* besides luck must have kept them safe. The lesson people learned was that nuclear deterrence works.

But a closer look at the facts of the various crises leads to a remarkable but undeniable conclusion: the conviction that nuclear deterrence makes crises more stable is not based on facts. Each of the five crises we'll look at in this chapter includes a moment when nuclear deterrence failed to restrain leaders from aggression. None of the failures led to nuclear war, but a number of them came perilously close. And taken together, they cast doubt on the notion that nuclear deterrence is the robust influencer of events that it is often depicted to be. In fact, nuclear deterrence looks like doubtful protection in a crisis. It *can* fail, and it *has* failed — many times.

Nuclear Deterrence

Deterrence is defined most economically by Glenn Snyder: "the power to dissuade." Alexander George and Richard Smoke define it as "the persuasion of one's opponent that the costs and/or risks of a given course of action . . . outweigh its benefits." Thomas Schelling calls deterrence "a threat . . . intended to keep an adversary from doing something."[1] It is a psychological process. Nuclear deterrence is a way of getting inside your adversary's head. According to deterrence theory, before leaders decide to go to war, they calculate what the likely costs of doing so would be. They think about the costs, then they think about the benefits. Deterrence works by persuading decision makers that the costs will be greater than the benefits. You remind your opponent of the death and destruction that would result from a war; your opponent realizes (you hope) that the costs are too great and then decides not to take aggressive action.

Of course, nuclear deterrence isn't the only kind of deterrence there is. Conventional weapons can be used for deterrence. In the 1920s, the French built the Maginot Line — an extremely strong set of fortifications along France's border with Germany — to both provide defense and act as a deterrent. The message the French were sending with the Maginot Line was this: *We're very well prepared for war, and any attack on us will be extremely costly.* (It didn't work.)

And deterrence isn't used just in war. Societies deter would-be criminals by punishing lawbreakers who are caught. Presumably, the more severe the punishment — like cutting off the hands of thieves — the more likely the deterrent will work. Parents deter their children from eating cookies that are cooling on the counter by threatening to spank them if they do. Encouraging people to count the costs of an action can work in any number of different settings.

Does non-nuclear deterrence work? It seems to. Children do behave most of the time. Most people resist the temptation to steal. And states often decide against war. But ordinary deterrence can also fail: sometimes children take cookies even after being warned; a surprising number of people break the law even though their friends are in jail; and history is replete with examples of states going to war despite knowing the costs will be high. So the effectiveness of ordinary deterrence varies from situation to situation: sometimes it works, sometimes not.

Nuclear deterrence, however, is presumed to be different. Ordinary deterrence may work only part of the time, but nuclear deterrence (it is assumed) is nearly perfect. Because the costs of nuclear war would be so frightful, nuclear deterrence is especially reliable, most people believe. Nuclear deterrence is a stop sign with a picture of nuclear war on it. We imagine that such a terrifying sign will undoubtedly work. But what we imagine doesn't always turn out to be true.

Cuban Missile Crisis

The Cuban missile crisis was a watershed in the history of nuclear weapons. The British historian A.J.P. Taylor called it "the two most important weeks in human history."[2] Robert Kennedy, the president's brother and the attorney general, said that the crisis brought the world to "the abyss of nuclear destruction and the end of mankind."[3] Kennedy later described one of the most intense moments in a memoir of the crisis:

> I think that these few minutes were the time of gravest concern for the President. Was the world on the brink of a holocaust? Was it our error? A mistake? Was there something further that should have been done? Or not done? His hand went up to his face

and covered his mouth. He opened and closed his fist. His face seemed drawn, his eyes pained, almost gray. We stared at each other across the table. For a few fleeting seconds, it was almost as though no one else was there and he was no longer the President.

Inexplicably, I thought of when he was ill and almost died; when he lost his child; when we learned that our oldest brother had been killed; of personal times of strain and hurt. . . .

We had come to the time of final decision. . . . I felt we were on the edge of a precipice with no way off. This time, the moment was now — not next week — not tomorrow, "so we can have another meeting and decide"; not in eight hours, "so we can send another message to Khrushchev and perhaps he will finally understand." No, none of that was possible. One thousand miles away in the vast expanse of the Atlantic Ocean the final decisions were going to be made in the next few minutes. President Kennedy had initiated the course of events, but he no longer had control over them.[4]

The lessons of the Cuban missile crisis loom large. According to scholar Richard Ned Lebow, they "occupy a central place both in United States foreign policy and in international relations theory."[5] The memory of this crisis — and of all the nuclear crises of the Cold War — profoundly shapes our thinking about nuclear weapons.

Most historians and policymakers tell the story of the crisis like this: Nikita Khrushchev (then premier of the Soviet Union) wanted to put nuclear missiles in Cuba; he was in the process of doing so when U.S. spy planes discovered what was going on. The United States imposed a naval blockade on Cuba; Khrushchev realized there was a real danger of nuclear war; he reversed course and withdrew the missiles. Told in this way, the story of the Cuban missile crisis is strong evidence that nuclear deterrence works.

But this ignores another perspective. Scholars, particularly in the West, focus on Khrushchev's actions and pay much less attention to those of the U.S. president. It takes two, after all, to make a crisis. It might be possible to build a case that Khrushchev was deterred by the danger of nuclear war. It is considerably more problematic to show that President Kennedy was.

On the morning of October 16, 1962, John F. Kennedy was informed that U.S. spy planes had discovered that Soviet medium-range nuclear missiles were secretly being placed in Cuba. The move violated no treaty, but the Soviet Union had explicitly denied that they were putting nuclear missiles in Cuba, and Kennedy had publicly warned that any offensive missiles in Cuba would raise the most serious issues for the United States.

Kennedy was already under a fair amount of political pressure about Cuba. All summer long, before anyone knew about the nuclear missiles, men and materiel had been arriving in Cuba, leading Republican congressmen to issue stinging condemnations of Kennedy and his administration. Kennedy, they said, was soft on Communism. The previous year, Kennedy had approved a CIA-planned invasion of Cuba by Cuban expatriates, but when the invasion went horribly wrong, he had refused to send U.S. forces to the rebels' aid. The Republican criticism hit deep. So even before the missiles were discovered, Cuba was a source of domestic political danger for Kennedy.

Once he was informed about the missiles, and after a week of secret deliberations with his advisers, Kennedy announced a "quarantine" of Cuba — a naval blockade to keep all further military supplies from reaching the island — and, in a dramatic, nationally televised address, he demanded that the missiles be removed. A very tense week followed, during which fear of nuclear war gripped the United States, Russia, Cuba, and the rest of the world. Eventually, the Soviet Union agreed to remove the missiles from Cuba in exchange for a public pledge by the United States that it would not invade Cuba. In private, Kennedy assured Khrushchev that — although it could not be acknowledged publicly as a trade — U.S. nuclear missiles close to the Soviet Union's border in Turkey would be removed.

But before we put the Cuban missile crisis in the Supports Nuclear Deterrence column, there is the question of the failure of nuclear deterrence to keep Kennedy from blockading Cuba. If fear of nuclear war prevents leaders from taking steps that might lead to nuclear war, and if Kennedy knew that blockading Cuba might result in nuclear war, then why wasn't *Kennedy* deterred?

Sir Michael Quinlan, a distinguished nuclear theorist in the United Kingdom, said, "Only a state ruler possessed by a reckless lunacy scarcely paralleled even in pre-nuclear history would contemplate with equanimity initiating a conflict that seemed likely to bring nuclear weapons down upon his country."[6] Most nuclear scholars and military officers who think about these matters agree: you'd have to be crazy to risk nuclear war. Yet isn't this exactly what Kennedy did?[7]

It might be argued that the risk of nuclear war was not as obvious when Kennedy acted as it was when Khrushchev was forced to withdraw. So let's begin by asking: How clear was it that Kennedy was initiating a crisis that might lead to nuclear war? First, as part of the exchange of rhetoric in the early fall, the Soviet Union had warned that war would result if Cuba was attacked:

> There is no need for the Soviet Union to shift its weapons for the repulsion of aggression, for a retaliatory blow, to any other country, for instance Cuba. . . . [The] Soviet Union has such powerful rockets to carry these nuclear warheads that there is no need to search for sites for them beyond the boundaries of the Soviet Union. . . . [One] cannot now attack Cuba and expect that the aggressor will be free from punishment. If this attack is made, this will be the beginning of the unleashing of war.[8]

Although the Soviets threatened only war, not nuclear war, some, at least, in Kennedy's administration took it to mean the latter. In his memoir, Kennedy's speechwriter and close aide Theodore Sorensen interpreted the threat as meaning "any U.S. military action against Cuba would unleash nuclear war."[9] Sorensen was probably right not to make much of the distinction between war and nuclear war: any conventional war over Cuba had a good chance of ending up as a nuclear war.

Could the Kennedy administration somehow have misread or wrongly discounted the possibility of nuclear war? This seems unlikely. Kennedy himself, after the crisis was over, remarked to Sorensen that he thought the chances of a war had been "somewhere between one out of three and even."[10] So the risk of nuclear war was clear in Kennedy's mind. But perhaps Kennedy appreciated the risks only after he had lived through them. It certainly makes sense that one would have a better understanding of the dangers after seeing them up close. Again, the evidence makes this explanation unlikely.

During the crisis, Kennedy met with fifteen advisers who later became known as the ExComm (the executive committee of the National Security Council). In the first six days of the crisis (that is, before a course of action was announced), the possibility of nuclear war growing out of the crisis was raised at least sixty times, with President Kennedy himself making the case for the severity of the risk in a conversation with the Joint Chiefs of Staff on Friday, October 19, 1962.[11] It seems clear that, although Kennedy's appreciation of the risk was probably more vivid and visceral once he had lived through the crisis, he was sufficiently aware of it going in that nuclear deterrence should have worked. It would have been obvious to anyone that either of the potential U.S. actions being discussed — blockade or air strike — could lead to nuclear war.

So why did nuclear deterrence fail? And why did Kennedy take steps that seem to meet Quinlan's definition of *reckless lunacy*?

One way that proponents of nuclear weapons explain Kennedy's willingness to risk nuclear war is by arguing that U.S. nuclear superiority made the risk of nuclear war negligible.[12] After it was all over, a number of the ExComm's members argued the importance of superiority.[13] As General Maxwell Taylor summed up the situation, "I was so sure we had 'em over a barrel, I never worried much about the final outcome."[14] But most of the senior participants and Kennedy himself said, either directly or indirectly, that nuclear superiority had had little to do with decisions made during the crisis.[15]

It's also not obvious that having more weapons was a clear advantage. Even though the numbers of missiles and bombers were weighted in favor of the United States, by the late 1950s both sides had the ability to inflict significant damage in the event of a war, even after absorbing a nuclear strike. As Kennedy's national security adviser McGeorge Bundy explained, "What we knew about Soviet nuclear forces at the time was simply that they were large enough to make any nuclear exchange an obvious catastrophe for Americans too. . . . The fact that our own strategic forces were very much larger gave us no comfort."[16]

Even assuming that the United States got in the first blow and destroyed many of the Soviet Union's nuclear weapons on the ground, the United States would still, according to studies at the time, suffer 100,000,000 casualties — more than half of its 187,000,000 population. While they were still behind in numbers of weapons, the Soviets had achieved parity in their ability to inflict devastation.[17]

The final piece of evidence about nuclear superiority's effect or non-effect on the crisis is that despite the fact that the Soviets were behind in numbers of missiles, this didn't translate into timidity.[18] At the height of the crisis, when the likelihood of war appeared to be greatest, Khrushchev suggested a potential solution by offering to remove the missiles in exchange for a no-invasion pledge from the United States. But twenty-four hours later, he proposed a different deal, this time offering to remove the missiles in exchange for both a no-invasion pledge *and* the removal of the U.S. missiles in Turkey. A negotiator in a dangerously inferior position rarely risks making new demands.

As historian Marc Trachtenberg concluded: "Actually, there is no evidence that President Kennedy and his advisers counted missiles, bombers and warheads, and decided on that basis to take a tough line. The veterans of the crisis have often denied that any calculation of that sort had been made, and there is no reason to dispute them on this point."[19]

Despite a clear risk of nuclear war, a risk he was fully aware of and that was not at all diminished by his larger arsenal, President John F. Kennedy chose to blockade Cuba. Nuclear deterrence, so often considered certain and reliable, failed. In the most dangerous nuclear crisis the world has ever known, one leader saw the nuclear deterrence stop sign, saw the horrifying image of nuclear war painted on it, and gunned through the intersection anyway.

Near Misses

Nuclear deterrence failed to stop Kennedy from blockading Cuba, but the crisis did not lead to nuclear war. That, however, is little comfort. Because more than once during the crisis, we came within a hairsbreadth of nuclear war.

Nuclear war could have broken out as a result of three events that did happen and one that easily could have: a U-2 spy plane that strayed over Soviet airspace at the height of the crisis; a Soviet submarine that was harassed with depth charges; a plane that was shot down over Cuba; and the planned invasion of Cuba by U.S. forces. Each of these events nearly ended in nuclear war, and in some cases, the use of nuclear weapons was averted only at the last possible moment.

Incredibly, on the day when the tensions of the Cuban missile crisis were greatest, Saturday, October 27, 1962, the guidance system on a U-2 spy plane malfunctioned. (Things always go wrong at the worst possible moment.) The plane was on a routine air-sampling mission over the North Pole. The outbound leg, from Alaska to the North Pole, was uneventful. But on the return leg, the plane veered eight hundred miles off course, going more than three hundred miles inside the Soviet Union. At the height of the crisis. The Soviets could easily have mistaken this plane for a bomber loaded with nuclear weapons.

Finally realizing the problem, the U-2 pilot turned back toward Alaska. Russian fighters scrambled to intercept and shoot down the intruder. American fighters scrambled to meet the U-2 and escort it back. But because of the looming possibility of war, earlier in the week, crews had removed the conventional weapons from U.S. fighters and replaced them with Falcon nuclear air-to-air missiles. A single Falcon missile could do extraordinary damage to incoming flights of bombers. But this meant that if U.S. and Soviet fighters tangled, the only ordnance the U.S. fighters had onboard were nuclear weapons. As luck would have it, the fighters did not intercept one another, and eventually the U-2 got safely home. But this routine air-sampling mission illustrates how easy it is for a series of unrelated errors and mishaps to spiral out of control into nuclear war.[20]

The seas around Cuba were also a potential site for confrontation between U.S. and Soviet forces. During the early fall of 1962, the Soviets had sent four Foxtrot-class attack submarines to patrol the waters near Cuba and keep a watchful eye over the many freighters carrying military materiel to that island. When the blockade was imposed, U.S. naval commanders were eager to find these submarines and force them to surface. U.S. officials had earlier sent a message to Moscow saying that as part of the blockade, they were going to force Soviet submarines to surface and identify themselves. They would do this by dropping nonlethal depth charges, they said. But Moscow either never received this message or failed to forward it to the captains of its subs in the Caribbean.

On Saturday, October 27, 1962, Valentin Savitsky, the captain of Soviet submarine B-59, was nearing the end of his tether. His vessel "was plagued with mechanical problems. The ventilation system had broken down. . . . Temperatures aboard ranged from

110–140 degrees. The presence of carbon monoxide was approaching critical levels." In addition, the U.S. Navy "had been chasing his submarine for the last two days. His batteries were dangerously low. He had been unable to communicate with Moscow for more than twenty-four hours. He had missed a scheduled radio session that afternoon because American airplanes had appeared overhead and he had been forced to make an emergency dive." He knew that the world was on the brink of war. Who knew what might have happened during the last two days while he was trying to avoid the Americans?

Now four U.S. destroyers were circling over B-59's position and dropping explosives into the water all around it. The explosions played on the nerves of the Soviet captain and his crew, down in the dim light and the heat of the submerged submarine. The sub was armed with twenty or so conventional torpedoes. But it also carried one nuclear torpedo with a ten-kiloton warhead. Authorization was needed from Moscow to use the nuclear torpedo, but there were no special locks or devices to prevent a captain from launching the torpedo on his own initiative.

As the explosions continued, Captain Savitsky summoned the officer in charge of the nuclear torpedo and told him to prepare it for firing. "Maybe the war has already started up there while we are doing somersaults down here," he shouted. "We're going to blast them now! We will perish ourselves, but we will sink them all! We will not disgrace our Navy!" Fortunately, cooler heads prevailed, and Savitsky was eventually convinced to bring B-59 to the surface without firing any torpedoes.[21] A missed warning about blockade procedures, accidents, mechanical failures, and the fraying nerves of sailors under stress; suddenly, there was only the flimsiest divide between a minor confrontation and nuclear war.

U.S. spy planes had been flying over Cuba continually since the crisis began. Initially, Soviet antiaircraft units refrained from shooting them down, but as the crisis heightened, it became more and more difficult to endure the overflights. Finally, General Issa

Pliyev, commander of all Soviet forces in Cuba, informed Moscow that he intended to shoot down any planes that came into Cuban airspace. On Saturday, October 27, while Pliyev was confined to bed because of an illness, his deputies noted an American spy plane taking pictures over eastern Cuba, and on their own authority, they ordered the plane shot down. Which it was.

President Kennedy and his advisers had worried about the risks of sending spy planes over Cuba. They had discussed it and agreed that they would continue the overflights because information was vital but that if any plane was shot down, they would respond immediately by attacking and destroying the SAM missile site that had downed the plane.

Now word arrived that an American pilot had been shot down over Cuba and was presumed dead. Sitting in the White House looking at one another, Kennedy and his advisers realized that their order had sent an American to his death. Kennedy's aides expected that the next step would be an immediate attack on a SAM antiaircraft battery in Cuba, an attack that could easily escalate into full-on combat. U.S. and Soviet aircraft might tangle over Cuba as the Soviets tried to prevent the attack on the SAM site. Soviet or Cuban aircraft might attack the blockading naval forces or sites in the United States. Once real fighting starts and more and more actors begin making decisions on their own, the ability of commanders to keep a situation in check ebbs away.

Kennedy, aware that the crisis could spiral out of control, postponed the counterstrike against the SAM battery. And the question of retaliation became moot when the crisis was resolved the following day.[22] In a crisis, even nonviolent activity—like gathering information—can seem threatening. And when people feel threatened, violence often follows.

Finally, the most troubling possibility for direct escalation to nuclear war comes from an action that might have been taken. If the United States had been unable to negotiate the removal of the Soviet missiles from Cuba, the plan was to invade Cuba and take the missiles out by force. This course of action carried with it enormous hidden dangers. What Kennedy and his advisers did not know was that any invasion of Cuba would have immediately touched off a nuclear war. Unbeknownst to U.S. intelligence officials, Soviet forces on Cuba included two batteries of tactical FKR nuclear cruise missiles, each equipped with forty nuclear warheads that were intended for use against any U.S. attack. In the opening hours of a U.S. invasion, these would have been used to destroy the U.S. forces at Guantánamo, any invasion flotilla as it neared shore, and any other targets of opportunity.

These examples clearly demonstrate that the Cuban missile crisis could easily have escalated into a nuclear war.[23] When nuclear deterrence fails, it brings the possibility of escalation — sometimes direct, sometimes indirect — to all-out nuclear war.

Given that the risk of starting a nuclear war failed to deter Kennedy, it is interesting to reflect on the lesson that he drew from the missile crisis. Afterward, he said, "Above all, while defending our own vital interests, nuclear powers must avert those confrontations which bring an adversary to a choice of either a humiliating retreat or a nuclear war."[24] It has always been assumed that Kennedy was talking about Khrushchev, that Khrushchev was the one facing humiliation or war. But a more interesting possibility exists. As Kennedy thought back over the crisis, it may have occurred to him that it was he who had run the risk of inciting nuclear war. Kennedy, after all, was the one who might have lost everything. In the long run, allowing the missiles into Cuba would not have done significant damage to the United States' reputation; the Soviets had survived having the United States put missiles in Turkey and Italy in 1961. But in the short run, if Kennedy had allowed the missiles to remain in Cuba, he would surely have lost his reelection bid in 1964. He might even have been, as he said to his brother during the height of the crisis, impeached for it. For Kennedy, the personal consequences of allowing missiles into Cuba would have been deeply humiliating. Everything that he had worked for his entire adult life would have been negated by this one event. Faced with the prospect of personal humiliation, of going down in history as a man defeated, Kennedy chose to risk nuclear war.

So what lessons should we learn from the Cuban missile crisis? On the one hand, you could argue that nuclear deterrence worked in getting Khrushchev to retreat. There was a threat of nuclear war, and the missiles were withdrawn. But you could also argue that deterrence may not have affected Khrushchev at all. Maybe Khrushchev agreed to withdraw because he valued the U.S. pledge not to invade Cuba. Maybe he was convinced by Robert Kennedy's secret promise that the Jupiter missiles would be removed from Turkey. Or it could be that he was swayed by the fact that the United States had conventional-military superiority in the Caribbean. So while it's possible that nuclear deterrence worked, it's also possible that nuclear deterrence had nothing to do with Khrushchev's decision to withdraw the missiles.

The failure of nuclear deterrence, on the other hand, is without doubt. Kennedy knew there was a risk of starting a nuclear war. He took actions that were irrevocable ("President Kennedy had initiated the course of events, but he no longer had control over them"). The blockade he ordered and the crisis that it engendered could have led to war, and, as we've seen, on a number of occasions nearly did. But this clear risk of nuclear war did not deter Kennedy.

Perhaps what is most striking about the Cuban missile crisis is the way in which it has been transformed from a failure of nuclear deterrence into proof that nuclear deterrence works well. The most important nuclear crisis to date provides clear evidence that nuclear deterrence can fail, and yet it is seen as the ultimate proof that deterrence works.

Berlin 1948

If the Cuban missile crisis were the only occasion when nuclear deterrence inexplicably failed, perhaps you could argue that one exception doesn't disprove the rule. But the evidence doesn't tell the story of a single exception. Again and again events that look like failures of nuclear deterrence crop up and quietly get ignored.

Let's return briefly to the Berlin crisis of 1948. Historians debate whether the redeployment of B-29s to England successfully deterred the Soviets.[25] But few ask how Stalin could have initiated the crisis in the first place. When he ordered access to Berlin cut off, the United States had a monopoly on nuclear weapons. (The Soviet Union would not explode its first nuclear weapon for another year.) Cutting off access to Berlin carried with it a significant risk of war. Where two large armed groups confront each other in a narrow space, there is always the possibility of accidental escalation. Or escalation could have been intentional. One of the options considered by Washington during the crisis was sending an armored column to force its way up the autobahn to Berlin. Given the risk of provoking a nuclear war and the U.S. nuclear monopoly, why wasn't Stalin deterred from initiating the blockade? If the risk of nuclear war deters, why did Stalin start a crisis that could have led to the use of nuclear weapons against his country?[26]

The failure here is not, in my judgment, as clear-cut as the failure in the Cuban missile crisis. The United States did not issue an explicit nuclear deterrence threat prior to the Berlin blockade. The rivalry between the United States and the Soviet Union was not yet as angry and intense as it would be in 1962. But what's striking about the episode is that it receives no attention in the literature. There are no journal articles exploring how or whether this nuclear deterrence failure can be explained. This lack of attention is peculiar. If the consequences of a failure are severe, wouldn't you want to carefully and conscientiously explore each possible suggestion of failure? Isn't this the way airline safety, for example, is treated? Each crash is investigated in excruciating detail. Yet possible failures of nuclear deterrence are left unexplored.

Korea

The implicit nuclear threat delivered during the Berlin crisis (by redeploying B-29s to Great Britain) has a fascinating counterpart in the Korean War. As we saw, although there is little evidence that the redeployment affected Soviet behavior one way or the other, in the years that followed, U.S. government officials came to believe that the threat during the Berlin crisis had had a significant impact.[27] Three weeks into the Korean War, therefore, B-29s were again redeployed to Great Britain. Presumably, they were intended to remind the Soviet Union that joining the Korean conflict could be risky.

As the situation in Korea continued to deteriorate, additional B-29s were dispatched to bases in the Pacific nearer the Korean theater. Remarkably, since military moves in wartime are generally carefully guarded secrets, this redeployment immediately found its way into the newspapers.

One could argue that the redeployment of bombers to England during the Korean War was intended to deter the Soviet Union from entering the war on the side of the North Koreans—and, since they did not enter the war, it worked. One could also argue that the redeployment of bombers to the Pacific was intended to warn the Chinese not to invade Taiwan—and that it worked. So you could take the history of the Korean War and tell it in such a way as to provide support for nuclear deterrence. But there is another angle from which this could be viewed. Since no explicit warning was issued to either the Russians or the Chinese, they were left to draw their own conclusions about what the redeployments meant. If the deployment to England was meant to warn the Soviets not to join the war, why wouldn't the deployment to the Pacific have been meant to warn China from coming in on the side of the North Koreans? This makes sense. The parallel is exact. And in this telling of the story, a dramatic failure of nuclear deterrence occurred, since the Chinese eventually entered the fighting in full force.

It isn't possible to know what motivated President Truman to send the bombers to the Pacific. What we do know is that the Chinese, in choosing to enter the war on the side of the North Koreans, ignored the risk of nuclear war. After the move of the nuclear-capable bombers was reported in the *New York Times,* prudence would have demanded that the Chinese consider the possibility that their siding with North Korea might result in the U.S. use of nuclear weapons against them. The opening of Chinese archives may one day show that they had sound reasons for believing that they were not risking nuclear attack. But for now, it certainly seems that they simply ignored the risk of nuclear war, which goes against the precepts of nuclear deterrence.[28] Again, this is not a very obvious failure of nuclear deterrence. The threat is entirely implicit. But the most troubling part about the episode is that it is not widely debated and discussed in deterrence literature.

Middle East War — 1973

In 1973, Israeli forces in the occupied territories were attacked by Syrian forces in the north and Egyptian forces in the south. Most of the scholarship about this crisis focuses on a worldwide alert of U.S. nuclear forces late in the crisis that was intended to discourage the Soviets from airlifting troops to Egypt. Most scholars believe, on balance, that the alert was effective — another case of using nuclear weapons to deter an opponent from making an unwanted foreign policy move. But this reading of the crisis overlooks a far more important issue.

In 1973, Israel was widely known to have a nuclear arsenal. Even though Israel refused to acknowledge it, the fact had been reported in a number of news outlets, including the *New York Times.* Yet neither Syria nor Egypt was deterred by this fact. How can this be? Syria and Egypt weren't contemplating risky steps in a crisis.

They were contemplating war. Surely the danger of a nuclear response by Israel should have figured into their calculations?

Nuclear weapons are usually seen as weapons of last resort. In a country as small as Israel — at its narrowest point, it is only 9.3 miles across — it doesn't take long for forces that break through the lines to threaten the survival of the nation. Why didn't the Syrians or the Egyptians fear that Israel would feel its survival was threatened? Where the last resort can arrive so quickly, doesn't it make sense for attackers to fear nuclear counterstrikes?

It's possible to think of a number of clever rationales for this failure of deterrence. But that is not the point. The point is that the failure hasn't been widely discussed. The nuclear alert by Kissinger at the end of the war has been extensively examined in the scholarly literature.[29] But the much more important failure of deterrence — and failing to deter a conventional war is a significant failure — hardly gets mentioned. Nuclear deterrence, the theory on which the security of millions of people is based, has a potentially serious flaw. Yet that flaw has not received close examination.

Gulf War

Finally, consider the Gulf War of 1990 to 1991. General Kevin Chilton, former commander of all U.S. strategic nuclear forces (Strat-Com), recently cited this episode as evidence that nuclear weapons are effective deterrents.[30] This is yet another example of how some facts are emphasized and others are elided. During the buildup to the Gulf War, U.S. secretary of state James Baker sent a letter to Iraq's leaders warning that if chemical or biological weapons were used during the conflict, the United States would respond with the "full measure of force." The letter was widely viewed as a nuclear threat and is often cited as a successful case of nuclear deterrence.

However, Secretary Baker's letter actually drew three red lines in the sand: Don't use chemical or biological weapons; don't set the oil wells on fire; don't make terrorist attacks against U.S. friends and allies. *Any one* of those three should have drawn the "full measure of force." While it is true that Iraqis did not use chemical or biological weapons, they *did* set the oil wells of Kuwait on fire, and they *did* launch Scud missile attacks at Israeli civilians. Two out of three red lines were crossed. If you set three goals for yourself and achieve one of them, do you say, "Well, *that* was an unmitigated success!"?

Conclusion

The history of nuclear deterrence has been distorted; certain episodes that might indicate failures of nuclear deterrence have been allowed to fade quietly into the background, while other episodes have been claimed as successes and given a prominence they may not deserve. Since the 1950s, the theory of deterrence and the school of thought it spawned have been enormously important in shaping the thinking of people who make decisions about foreign policy. Robert Jervis called it "probably the most influential school of thought in the American study of international relations."[31] But it may be that the very power of that school of thought has had a negative impact on our ability to see the facts. Richard Ned Lebow has looked closely at the effect of a strong theory on factual investigation.

Philosophers of science have observed that scientists tend to fit data into existing frameworks even if the framework does not do justice to the facts. Investigators deduce evidence in support of theory. Theory, once accepted, determines to which facts they pay attention. According to Thomas Kuhn, the several fields of science are each dominated by a "paradigm," an accepted body of related concepts that establishes the framework for research. The paradigm determines the phenomena that are important and what kinds of explanations "make sense." It also dictates the kinds of facts and explanations that are to be ignored because they are outside the paradigm or not relevant to the problem the paradigm has defined as important. Paradigms condition investigators to reject evidence that contradicts their expectations, to misunderstand it, to twist its meaning to make it consistent, to explain it away, to deny it, or simply to ignore it.[32]

It seems plain that something like this has happened with the Cold War crises discussed here. Uncomfortable facts have been ignored, and the parts of these crises that tend to reinforce the notion that nuclear deterrence works are brought front and center. The debate about nuclear deterrence appears to have left important facts out, to have presumed a unanimity of success that doesn't exist.[33]

Deterrence — ordinary deterrence — sometimes fails even when the consequences are severe. In a number of countries, thieves are punished by having their hands cut off. But people still steal. In China, government officials have been put to death for corruption. But corruption persists. At the outset of World War I, it was apparent that the war would engulf an entire continent. Despite this, people found ways to talk themselves into launching the war. In other words, ordinary deterrence works some of the time, but it also — some of the time — fails.

Nuclear theorists claim that nuclear deterrence is more reliable than ordinary deterrence. They claim it is a special case that works almost every time. But the evidence does not back them up. The record of Cold War crises shows that nuclear deterrence is not foolproof. This is serious, because if we are to rely on nuclear deterrence, it has to be perfect.[34] It's not enough for nuclear deterrence to work pretty well. It's not acceptable for it to work most of the time. Because any one failure might lead to a catastrophic, all-out nuclear war, nuclear deterrence has to be 99.9 percent reliable. One could even argue that if millions of people around the world are to risk their safety and security on nuclear deterrence, it had better work *every* time. Yet these Cold War crises present evidence that nuclear deterrence has failed on several occasions. This is deeply troubling. The bulletproof vest, it turns out, is made of cheesecloth.

The lessons that people learned from the Cold War crises — that nuclear weapons promote stability and that nuclear deterrence works reliably — don't seem to be well supported by the facts. They seem more like wishful thinking than carefully verified findings. If nuclear deterrence failed in a number of Cold War crises, then it seems possible that nuclear deterrence is no more reliable than ordinary deterrence. If nuclear deterrence can easily fail, the decision to rely on nuclear deterrence for safety and security is a reckless, foolish choice.

Myth 4

NUCLEAR WEAPONS KEEP US SAFE

WHAT IS TO BE MADE of the extended period since World War II in which no major wars have been fought? The United States and the Soviet Union squared off for more than forty-five years without coming to blows. And during that same time, Europe has known a period of remarkable peace — at least, compared with some periods in its turbulent history. What, people ask themselves, does this anomalous period of peace mean? Is it simply a stroke of luck? Has human nature changed? Or is there some change in the material factors that influence decisions about war?

One obvious possibility, particularly for those people who believe that nuclear weapons create stability in a crisis, is that nuclear weapons create stability in general, that they somehow promote peace on a larger scale. Nuclear deterrence not only coerces and dissuades, they assert, it prevents major wars as well.

This argument seems to make a certain amount of sense, and many people take the peace that's been experienced over the past sixty years as significant proof of the power of nuclear deterrence. But there are problems. First, proving something by using the absence of something else is trickier than it appears. Second, there are other factors that can adequately account for this period of peace. And finally, it turns out that there was another period of extended peace in Europe during which the major powers fought few wars. But in the end, that period of peace didn't prove anything.

The Long Peace

Historian John Lewis Gaddis argued forcefully that nuclear weapons were responsible for the peace over the previous decades in a watershed article in *International Security* in 1986 entitled "The Long Peace" and a subsequent book by the same name.[1] Gaddis argued that since no major war had been fought between the United States and the Soviet Union over the forty-one years from 1945 to 1986, and since no other explanation for this lack of war seemed persuasive, this constituted real evidence that nuclear deterrence both worked and was a crucial factor in keeping the peace. In other words, the "Long Peace" can be accounted for only by the existence of nuclear weapons. Since Gaddis published that work, the length of time has been extended to more than sixty-five years.

Gaddis builds his argument out of a series of subarguments. He talks about the fact that a bipolar system, with two great powers, is inherently more stable than one with three or more great powers. He argues that the classical liberal theory of close economic ties and cultural exchanges preventing war isn't true and therefore can't account for the lack of war. He argues that internal political or economic factors could not have been the cause of the "Long Peace." He points to a long list of crises that he asserts would typically have led to war but didn't, and he draws inferences about the inhibiting effect of nuclear arsenals. He concludes that "nuclear deterrence is the most important behavioral mechanism that has sustained the post–World War II international system."[2]

Describing the experience of Europeans and Americans as

a "Long Peace" makes sense. Those years have not been a time of unbroken peace for everyone, however. There was a decade of war after the breakup of Yugoslavia. Two major powers (the United States and China) did fight each other during the Korean War. There have been minor border wars between nuclear powers as well. There was a clash between Soviet and Chinese forces in 1969 and a series of crises between India and Pakistan. It's also worth remembering that in the world beyond Europe and Asia, there has been considerable violence. A decadelong civil war in the Congo left over a million people dead, and genocide in Cambodia and Rwanda killed millions more. This violence is sometimes overlooked by Europeans and Americans, who talk easily about "sixty-seven years of peace." But Gaddis is generally correct: there has been no major war, no World War III, over the past seventy years.

Gaddis is not alone. Many social scientists, government officials, students of international relations, and others believe that the evidence of the past decades is clear evidence of an important change.[3] Many people take the "Long Peace" as strong evidence that nuclear deterrence works to prevent major wars. It can be accounted for only by the existence of nuclear weapons, they say.[4] However, despite the fact that the peace over the past sixty-seven years is striking, there are a number of reasons to view this argument skeptically.

Virgins in the Volcano

One problem with taking many decades of peace as proof that deterrence works is that it is a proof by absence. Proof by absence is generally unreliable because it is so hard to nail down. There are any number of ways to prove an assertion: by deductive logic from a set of assumptions, by inductive logic from examples, by analogy to a similar situation, and so on. Proof by absence is particu-

larly difficult because it can be true only if there are no other possible causes for the end result. I assert that Mary ate the last cookie.
What I say is true if and only if Mary was the only person to have
been in the kitchen when the last cookie disappeared. If anyone
else was in the kitchen, or could have been in the kitchen, the proof
fails. Or if a squirrel could have gotten in and eaten the cookie. And
so on. Because life is so inherently multivariate, because each event
has so many things that might have caused it, proof by absence is
very demanding. It is, generally, the proof of last resort, used only
when no better forms of evidence are available.

And proof by absence is particularly subject to abuse. It's hard
to prove exactly what caused something *not* to happen, so unscrupulous or unrigorous people sometimes use proof by absence to
"prove" peculiar things. Consider the (imaginary) example of the
virgins in the volcano. One year the volcano erupts. People are appalled. The next year, a religious leader tells them that to keep the
volcano god happy, they have to throw a virgin into the volcano.
They do it, the volcano doesn't erupt that year, and the religious
leader triumphantly points to the "proof" that throwing a virgin in
"controlled" the volcano. Now they throw a virgin into the volcano
every year, and every year that the volcano doesn't erupt, they nod
their heads and say that the absence of eruption proves that sacrificing virgins works.[5]

The example is fanciful, but not unfair. Proof by absence is not
accepted in modern societies in any situation where serious matters are at stake. Take medicine, for example. Imagine that someone claimed to have discovered a new drug that prevents mesothelioma, a rare form of cancer. To prove this claim, the discoverer
carefully documented administering the drug to one hundred people and followed their health. After five years, none of them had
developed mesothelioma. The absence of cancer in the patients is
real. But would the U.S. Food and Drug Administration or any accredited medical organization take this as proof that the drug prevents mesothelioma?

Because people's lives are at stake, governments have instituted elaborate procedures for testing any new drug. Extensive, stringent double-blind testing on thousands of patients is required before a drug is approved for widespread use. Governments instituted these laws because in a life-or-death situation, proof by absence is not good enough.

Similarly, people take airline safety very seriously. Rigorous maintenance and testing are standard in almost every part of the world. Imagine that a woman comes up with a device that she claims prevents metal fatigue, a condition that affects aging aircraft. It works, she says, by a previously unknown property of sonic waves. Because she has a friend at the Federal Aviation Administration in the United States, ten of the devices are put on planes for a year. At the end of the year, none of the planes has crashed because of metal fatigue. The woman goes on TV and claims success. The absence of plane crashes proves her device works, she says. If an airline announced that it was going to stop its current metal-fatigue maintenance and testing and rely instead on these devices, would you fly that airline?

The fact that there has been no major war between the great powers or in Europe for more than sixty-seven years is *some* kind of proof. It counts for something. But you wouldn't want to rely on it if your life was on the line. We don't accept proof by absence in medicine, airline safety, or any other situation in which the risk of serious injury is present. And with good reason. It's unreliable proof. Why would anyone imagine it is acceptable proof where the lives of millions are at stake?

Other Reasons

For proof by absence to work, all other possible causes to explain the outcome have to be identified and ruled out. In the case of the "Long Peace," it turns out there are many other plausible reasons why there has been no war. Take five obvious ones.

1. EXHAUSTION AND DISTRACTION

The Russians lost an estimated twenty-seven million people during World War II. Something like 30 to 40 percent of their industrial capacity was destroyed. Is it any wonder that they were disinclined to fight a war for at least twenty or thirty years afterward? Additionally, both the United States and Russia were absorbed by a series of distractions that might have made fighting a war unattractive. Beginning in 1979, the Soviet Union was involved in the war in Afghanistan, which occupied upwards of a hundred thousand troops over the next nine years. The Soviet Union was disrupted by rapid turnover in its leadership (Andropov and Chernenko) in the early 1980s. In 1982, oil prices collapsed, putting a serious strain on the Soviet economy (some observers believe this was a central reason the Soviet Union dissolved in 1989).

The United States also experienced a series of distractions. Beginning in the late 1950s, civil rights protests absorbed the nation's attention and energies, and continued to do so for more than a decade. From 1964 to 1968, urban riots erupted each summer in various U.S. cities. Starting in 1965, the United States was engaged for a decade in a war in Vietnam. At the height of the conflict, five hundred thousand troops were deployed there.

2. CLOSER ECONOMIC TIES

Although Gaddis pooh-poohs closer economic ties as an explanation for peace, the economic integration going on in Europe is unprecedented in history. An area that historically was the engine of so many wars has become, under the European Union, more like a federation of states or even a single, loosely integrated state than a collection of sovereign nations. This extraordinary integration has surely affected the likelihood of war in Europe, the arena where the United States and Russia were most likely to come into conflict.

3. ALLIANCES

Europe has also been the site of two of the largest and most stable sets of alliances the world has ever known. Both NATO and the Warsaw Pact were remarkable in size, extent of integration, and longevity. Even if nuclear weapons had never existed, the presence of these large, robust alliances would have had an inhibiting effect on countries' decisions to go to war.

4. INTERNATIONAL TREATIES AND ORGANIZATIONS

There are, as well, more international organizations and treaties in the post–World War II world than ever before. The United Nations is a constant force for peace and international cooperation. And, increasingly, nations are bound together by treaties on ocean use, air pollution, trade, and a host of other common concerns. It is easy to denigrate the effectiveness of these treaties and organizations, but a plausible case can be made that they have had a moderating effect on decisions about war or peace.

5. PERIODS OF PEACE

Finally, sometimes there are simply periods of peace in history. From 1815 to 1848, there were thirty-three years of comparative peace in Europe that was not the result of nuclear weapons. The ancient Egyptians enjoyed two hundred years of uninterrupted peace. No Latin American countries have fought each other for seventy years. Given that periods of peace are not that anomalous, should we rush to find extraordinary explanations for the lack of war between the United States and Russia? Isn't it possible that the

current peace is just one of the periods of peace that humankind
has experienced at different times?

The Better Angels

Another important problem with the "Long Peace" argument is illustrated by the recent work of Harvard psychology professor Steven Pinker in his book *The Better Angels of Our Nature: Why Violence Has Declined*. Essentially a grand defense (in seven hundred
pages) of the liberal tradition, its main point is that the "artifices of
civilization have moved us in a noble direction."[6] The book is filled
with statistical information and interesting arguments. Pinker's assertion that violence overall has declined during the course of history is supported by a good deal of compelling evidence.

In the chapter devoted to the "Long Peace," Pinker says that the
long period of peace since World War II is the result not of nuclear
weapons but of progressive changes in human institutions. Pinker
may be right. Arguments about progressive change are outside the
scope of this book. But some people take Pinker's argument and
extrapolate from it that nuclear weapons issues no longer matter. In a world where war is unlikely, they say, why give these out-
moded weapons of the past a second thought? If people are gradually giving up violence, then no one needs to worry about nuclear
weapons. They will go out of existence of their own accord. But
there are three problems with this sort of complacent thinking.
First, Pinker carefully — and correctly — emphasizes that he is talking about a long-term trend. Progress can be a jagged line with fre-
quent spikes of violence, even if the overall trend is sloping slowly
down. Pinker does not claim that wars, even catastrophic wars, are
no longer possible.

Second, much of Pinker's book deals with violence in general —
rape, murder, and other interpersonal mayhem — not violence between states. Even where he analyzes war, he mixes in data about
civil war, revolution, and even genocide. This tends to support

his conclusions about violence in general but makes conclusions about wars between states more difficult to draw.[7]

Third, a good deal of the evidence he uses to make his point comes from the past sixty years. Pinker notes that there has been a remarkable falloff in the number and severity of wars during that time. No major war like World War II has been fought, and the number of smaller wars has declined as well. In addition, he points to data that seem to show that democracies are less prone to fight wars with other democracies.

Although I am persuaded by some of Pinker's general arguments, I am less persuaded by the argument he makes about the "Long Peace." The problem I have is encapsulated by the disagreement Pinker has with Arnold Toynbee. Toynbee was a well-known British historian whose twelve-volume *A Study of History* examined the rise and fall of civilizations. Toynbee was famously pessimistic on the question of whether more violent wars were likely in the future. Since Pinker is a Pulitzer Prize–winning psychologist, and since people often employ their strongest suits, perhaps it is not surprising that Pinker chides Toynbee based on psychology. Pinker says that in being pessimistic about the likelihood of war, Toynbee fell prey to a fallacy that cognitive psychologists call the availability heuristic. The availability heuristic argues that people base judgments on what they remember and that they tend to remember a limited set of striking examples, or perhaps what happened to them most recently, rather than complete sets of all the data. Toynbee believed more violent wars were likely, Pinker says, because he was writing in the 1950s, and the event that stood out most in his mind was the recent catastrophe of World War II.[8]

Pinker is one of the most influential science writers in the world today, and his psychology credentials are impressive. But if Toynbee were here to defend himself, he might chide Pinker in return, using his — Toynbee's — strongest suit. One of Toynbee's strengths as a historian was that he wrote about the great sweep of history; he didn't specialize in particular eras. As a historian,

Toynbee would have known what historians know best, which is that history is long. Conclusions that seem to make sense in one era are often invalidated in another. Historians learn humility from history because the complexity and scope of it reminds them that what is true in one era rarely applies across history's entire length.

The problem with Pinker's admonition of Toynbee and with his conclusions about the "Long Peace" is that war appears to be long. War, we know, has been a constant accompaniment to human existence throughout recorded human history. And there is significant archaeological evidence that group violence goes back beyond our earliest written records. So the phenomenon we are dealing with covers at least six thousand years. A trend has to begin somewhere, and the first evidence of a trend can sometimes be a dramatic break from the past. But basing large-scale conclusions on sixty years of evidence means basing conclusions on 1 percent of the evidence. You're claiming to have detected a trend based on 1 percent of the data. Particularly when one is dealing with a phenomenon that is apparently deeply rooted in human nature, this seems incautious. Toynbee would have had the humility to know that 1 percent of the evidence doesn't make a trend.

The "Long Peace" feels long to us because it is part of our immediate history. It is the experience of our parents' and grandparents' generations. But the past sixty years make up quite a short period in terms of human history. The "Long Peace" is actually a "short peace" in relation to the history of war. Making too much of the "Long Peace" risks falling into the fallacy of the availability heuristic. Pinker is right that progress toward peace tends to be a jagged line with spikes of war. The downward trend appears only over the longest time scale. Short-term spikes of war are still possible and even likely. He is also right that we cannot say that another major war will never come. To form judgments about long-term phenomena based on short-term evidence is not sound thinking.

The Victorians

One of the strongest reasons to be cautious about drawing conclusions from the past seventy or so years of peace is that people have made predictions based on periods of peace before. Those predictions were confident and backed by compelling statistical evidence. They were put forward by earnest, intelligent, and well-intentioned people. And they were profoundly wrong.

In the late 1890s and the early 1900s, the Victorians experienced their own long peace.

> In Europe in the ninety-nine years between the Battle of Waterloo and the First World War, most wars were short. The Seven Weeks War was one of the most remarkable events of that century but it was only one of a growing list of short wars. In the 1880s came an even shorter war, a fierce fortnight of fighting between Serbia and Bulgaria. In the 1890s Greece and Turkey fought near their hilly border, and many foreign correspondents barely had time to reach the battlefront before they were cabling home the news that the thirty days war had ended.[9]

In trying to understand this phenomenon, in trying to account for this strange break from the familiar rhythm of the past, the Victorians reached for a technological explanation. The new machines of the industrial age, they decided — steam-powered ships, trains, and telegraphs — were transforming war. New weapons were making long wars a thing of the past. Even before the lightning Prussian victories in 1866 and 1870, people had come to believe that industrial progress had made long, destructive wars impossible.

They also believed that changes in the world of commerce and finance made devastating wars much less likely. Banking and finance were viewed as "a delicate mechanism" that could not survive a long war. Similarly, experts pointed out that European nations were more commercially intertwined than they had ever been. Long wars were impossible, they said, because the disruption to commerce would limit the endurance of states.

Finally, many of the most serious of the Victorian intellectuals believed that peace had come to Europe because Europe was experiencing a flowering of civilization — a liberalizing of attitudes and values that exempted Europe from the baser sorts of human behavior, like war. According to one historian, "What made the peace that followed 1815 more than a mere halt was largely the culture, the customs, laws and manners, which had evolved in Europe and had found strong and influential expression in the great philosophical, literary and artistic works of the eighteenth century."[10]

The shortness of the wars that had occurred seemed to them to be "evidence that Europe's warlike spirit was ebbing."[11] To the Victorians, the trend toward peace and away from war seemed clear. As late as 1911, Sir Thomas Barclay, an authority on international law, could write in the *Encyclopedia Britannica* that the prospects for peace were good. Progress was being made in America, he declared. The fact that armies were drilling throughout Europe was not disturbing because citizens were learning obedience as well as war. The number of conferences on peace and international agreements led him to prophesy that war would eventually be eliminated. War "is coming, among progressive peoples, to be regarded merely as an accidental disturbance of that harmony and concord among mankind which nations require for the fostering of their domestic welfare."[12]

As the turn of the nineteenth century approached, Victorians in Europe congratulated themselves on their civility and good manners. There might be wars in the colonies (fighting savages), they said, but there would never be savage war again in Europe. We have evolved too far, they said; our commercial interests are too intertwined, we are too educated, too *cultured* for the sort of brutal, rampaging war that engulfed all of Europe during the 1600s or in the Napoleonic era. Massive wars like that, they confidently and complacently asserted, are gone forever.

Current pronouncements about peace and progress eerily echo the words of these long-dead Victorians. Today, some scholars and even government officials say that the world has definitively changed. Wars will no longer be fought, and our only concerns are terrorism and civil war. A French scholar of nuclear weapons, for example, claims to perceive a fundamental change in the attitudes of states: "Most modern states have less tolerance for human suffering and destruction than was the case until 1945."[13] A British general points to the absence of wars with large tank battles and declares, "[T]he wars in which armoured formations could and should be used are no longer practical. This does not mean a big fight with large groups of forces and weapons is no longer possible, but it does mean that it will not be an industrial one in either intent or prosecution; industrial war no longer exists."[14] On all sides, there are confident pronouncements that long, destructive wars will not — *cannot* — come again.

The Victorians (like us) believed they knew why there had been such an extended period of peace. Here is historian Geoffrey Blainey:

> Those living in the three generations after Waterloo had wondered at the long peace and sought explanations in events that were happening simultaneously. They noticed that international peace coincided with industrialism, steam engines, foreign travel, freer and stronger commerce and advancing knowledge. As they saw specific ways in which these changes could further peace, they concluded that the coincidence was causal. Their explanation, however, was based on one example or one period of peace. They ignored earlier if shorter periods of peace experienced by a Europe which had no steam trains, few factories, widespread ignorance and restricted commerce.[15]

The Victorians dreamed they had achieved peace. The single most famous (and ironic) of these Victorians is actually an

Edwardian: Norman Angell, a British MP whose 1910 book *The Grand Illusion* was an international bestseller. Just four years before the "war to end all wars," Angell argued that the economies of Europe's various nations had become so entwined and interdependent as to render war obsolete. It turned out Angell was right: there was an enormous illusion haunting Europe. But it was not the illusion he had in mind. The incredible ferocity of World War I — the senseless slaughter of millions, the dehumanizing brutality of trench warfare, the horror of gas and massed artillery barrages and machine guns — tore the Victorians' pretensions and complacency asunder. They found themselves confronted by a human reality that was not so cultured and peaceloving after all.

Even a cursory review of the facts shows that the lust for war ebbs and flows throughout history. We appear to be sailing through a period of relative calm now, with less destruction and less killing than there was seventy years ago. But these sorts of calms have come before. Human beings have demonstrated, time and again, an appetite for war that does not seem to fade or wear itself out. The desire for war — and the destruction and killing that go with it — seems to be a savagery that only sleeps.

Emotion and War

Proponents of nuclear weapons often talk about the way in which these weapons keep a lid on aggressive tendencies. It is certainly true that various leaders have talked about the fear they felt when confronted with the reality of nuclear war. There is evidence that the risks of bringing on such a destructive war have *some* effect. But what kind of effect? How long does it last? Is it possible that a leader could talk himself or herself into fighting a nuclear war? Many leaders have launched wars that sober historians later judged to be simple folly. Is that kind of folly possible in a world with nuclear weapons?[16]

Robert Kennedy was an expert of sorts on nuclear war. He sat in meetings during the Cuban missile crisis where nuclear war was discussed and almost certainly thought about the very real possibility of his brother having to order the launch of U.S. nuclear weapons. Robert Kennedy was a passionate, serious, thoughtful man. He was one of only a handful of people who actually participated in a nuclear crisis. What did he think about this question of human folly? What did his experience lead him to conclude about this issue of emotion and war?

Here is an excerpt from his 1968 presidential campaign book called *To Seek a Newer World,* written five years after the Cuban missile crisis.

Those who disparage the threat of nuclear weapons ignore all evidence of the darker side of man, and of the history of the West — our history. Many times the nations of the West have plunged into inexplicable cataclysm, mutual slaughter so terrible and so widespread that it amounted nearly to the suicide of a civilization. The religious wars of the sixteenth century, the Thirty Years' war in the seventeenth century, the terrible excesses that followed the French Revolution — these have been equaled and grotesquely outmatched in the modern twentieth century.

Twice within the memory of living men, the nations of Europe, the most advanced and cultured societies of the world, have torn themselves and each other apart for causes so slight, in relation to the cost of struggle, that it is impossible to regard them as other than excuses for the expression of some darker impulse. Barbara Tuchman reminds us that the people of Europe were *relieved* at the outbreak of World War I: "Better a horrible ending than a horror without end," said people in Germany. "Is not peace an element of civil corruption," asked the great writer Thomas Mann, and war "a purification, a liberation, an enormous hope?" Englishmen cheered the news of war's outbreak all day and night, and Rupert Brooke wrote:

> *Now God be thanked Who has matched us with*
> *His hour*

Honour has come back
And we have come into our heritage.

Perhaps only in Germany was similar enthusiasm to greet renewed combat in 1939. But the damage of this second war was greater, especially to noncombatants. The camps and ovens, the murders and mutual inhumanities of the Eastern front, the unrestricted bombing of cities (with deliberate concentration on areas of workers' housing), the first use of atomic bombs — truly this was war virtually without rules or limits. Its most important lesson for us is perhaps that we have no real explanation for it. We can explain how war broke out. We can understand our own response to the Nazi threat. But we have no reason for the fantastic disproportion between the combatants' war aims and the things that were done, none perhaps but the wrath of war described by Achilles in Book XVIII of the *Iliad,*

> *"that makes a man go mad for all his*
> *goodness of reason,*
> *That rage that rises within and swirls like*
> *smoke in the heart and becomes in our madness*
> *a thing more sweet than the dripping of honey."*

The destruction of the two World Wars was limited only by technology. Now nuclear weapons have removed that limit. Who can say that they will not be used, that a rational balance of terror will restrain emotions we do not understand? Of course, we have survived into the third decade of the Atomic Age. Despite many limited wars and crises before 1914, Europe had known substantial peace for a century — and at its end saw war as deliverance. Nuclear war may never come, but it would be the rashest folly and ignorance to think that it will not come because men, being reasonable beings, will realize the destruction it would cause.[17]

There is little reason to think that the past seventy years represent a watershed in civilization or that human nature has suddenly and decisively evolved. There is even less reason to think that nuclear weapons are responsible for this period of peace. The fear of catastrophic war has probably contributed to this long period of peace in some way. But to make the leap from nuclear weapons having "contributed in some way" to the assertion that nuclear weapons preserve the peace and will prevent World War III in perpetuity is to ignore the evidence of history. If we are responsible, we must admit that we do not know what effect nuclear weapons have on human beings when it comes to decisions about war. Until we can be completely certain that nuclear weapons ensure peace, it is reckless to risk the lives of millions of people on a hunch.

Myth 5

THERE IS NO ALTERNATIVE

THE FINAL MYTH I want to address didn't grow out of experiences but was extrapolated from the other four myths. Once people believed that nuclear weapons had a unique ability to shock opponents, were certain to be decisive in war, created a special kind of deterrence that worked powerfully and reliably, and kept the peace, they went on to draw other conclusions. They determined that nuclear weapons could not be gotten rid of because they couldn't be disinvented, that the importance of nuclear weapons was proved by their acknowledged role in international relations, and that even if there were problems with the historical events that had elevated nuclear weapons to their current position, now that their aura of invincibility had been established, they could never be done away with. None of these arguments makes sense in light of the collapse of the other four myths. Let's examine each one in turn.

The Genie

The best and strongest argument for keeping nuclear weapons is what I call the genie argument. The genie shows up all the time in the discussion about making a world free of nuclear weapons.[1] A nuclear proponent listens to liberals complain and then says, "Yes, they're dangerous. But I don't know how you can ever get rid of them." Then, with a sad, knowing shake of the head: "You just can't disinvent nuclear technology." Or, more colorfully, recalling the story of Aladdin and the magic lamp: "You can't stuff the nuclear genie back into the bottle!"

The thing that makes this argument so compelling is that it is absolutely true. You can't disinvent technology. With the rare exception of certain arcane techniques now lost because they were known to only a few (like the carefully guarded secret for tinting medieval stained glass a particularly spectacular shade of red), technologies never die. So the argument that nuclear weapons can never be disinvented is absolutely true. It also happens to be absolutely irrelevant.

No technology is *ever* disinvented. Technology doesn't go away because it's disinvented. It goes away because other technology replaces it. Or it simply falls out of use because it was bad technology. For example, think about early bicycles with one giant wheel in the front and one small wheel in the back. Called penny-farthings in some parts of the world, these contraptions were difficult to ride and dangerous to fall from. Yet no one nodded knowingly and warned, *You'll never be able to stuff the penny-farthing genie back into the bottle!* When better bicycles came along, with two tires the same size, the penny-farthing simply fell out of use.

These bikes were called penny-farthings in some places.

Or consider this piece of remarkable technology. The perambu-

In the English town of Hextable in Kent, 1938.

lator shown here was built with a gas-mask filter attached so that Junior could breathe comfortably while the nanny took him for a stroll during a chemical weapons attack. This technology did not have to be disinvented. For some reason, it never really caught on.

Finally, take a look at the amazing flying platform developed by the U.S. military. The Hiller VZ-1 Pawnee was invented in 1953, and six prototypes were made. The craft was remarkably stable, although it could not fly very high. I call it the Here-I-am-totally-vulnerable-without-protection-or-anywhere-to-hide Death Platform. The Pawnee never went into full-scale production. In order for technology to lose its appeal, it is never necessary to disinvent it.

I suspect that this argument about technology comes from a myth. The role that technology

The Hiller VZ-1 was a one-person flying platform that hovered ten to fifteen feet off the ground.

plays here sounds very much like the evil spirits in the story of Pandora's box. Once an idea for new technology has been developed, once it's out of the box, then — like the evil spirits in the story — it can never be controlled or limited. Pandora opened the box, the demons escaped, and sadness and evil could not be cleansed from the world. But technological inventions are not evil spirits. They are implements that are either useful or not. If the technology works, if it is useful, then we keep it around. When it stops being useful, it slides into oblivion without even the slightest push from us.

The genie argument is no more than a clever debater's trick. It uses a true but irrelevant statement to distract from the real issue. The real question is whether nuclear weapons are useful — not whether they are like evil spirits in some age-old myth. If nuclear weapons are useful, then we have to keep them. It's as simple as that. If they provide real security that cannot be had any other way, and if the security they provide outweighs the danger they create, then we must accustom ourselves to having them around. But if they are not very useful, if they are simply large, dangerous, clumsy explosives that spread poison downwind and have very few real applications, then we need to undertake an entirely new discussion.

Even though it's irrelevant, the genie argument is still important. It matters because it is psychologically suggestive. It tells us something about the way that proponents of nuclear weapons see the world. In their eyes, nuclear weapons are *magic*. Nuclear weapons are like a genie that can grant your every wish. Bring your nuclear weapon out, wave it around, and people will do whatever you say.[2] Nuclear weapons are extraordinary, it is claimed; they have power that goes far beyond conventional weapons'. They are, Stimson said, *psychological* weapons with a unique ability to shock and awe. It is not just the physical capabilities of nuclear weapons that matter, say their proponents. What makes them special is their remarkable aura. But if you stop and think about it, special auras and unique abilities to shake the human psyche sound more like voodoo and incantation than a weapons system. Proponents apparently really mean it when they talk about a magic genie.

But nuclear weapons are not magic. They are tools, and like any other tool, they are controlled by us. We decide when to use them. It seems peculiar to have to say it, but the weapons themselves lack volition. We don't have to fear that they will go off by themselves; we only have to fear that *we* will go off half-cocked. Genies, famously, have their own thoughts and intentions and often willfully misinterpret their owners' wishes. Nuclear weapons can't act that way. They can't act at all.

Like the usefulness of any tool, the usefulness of nuclear weapons depends on the circumstances of their use. Tools are situational. The question you ask yourself when approaching a task is not *Do I have the biggest tool possible?* but *Do I have the right tool for the job?* The two key questions for nuclear weapons are: When are nuclear weapons the right tool for the job? And how likely are these circumstances to arise? These are the sorts of questions that would be asked in a pragmatic investigation rather than one based on mythology.

Currency of Power

Proponents of nuclear weapons might say, "You keep asserting that nuclear weapons are not as powerful as we think, but doesn't the fact that respected experts and leaders call nuclear weapons the ultimate weapon count for something? How is it possible that so many important people could be wrong? Think about all the American presidents, British prime ministers, and Russian premiers (to name only a few) who have asserted the centrality of nuclear weapons. And what about the Iranians? They appear to be working hard to get nuclear weapons. They seem to think nuclear weapons have some value. The North Koreans suffered through incredible hardships and sanctions to fulfill their nuclear ambitions.

If nuclear weapons aren't worth it, then why do all these people say they are and — more important — act as if they are?"

The problem is that we live in groups. Every group needs an object that can conveniently serve as a token or stand-in for some other item (perhaps a somewhat abstract or intangible thing) that has value. In a group, we treat these value-tokens as if they were the real thing. We handle them and use them every day. And as a result of the seductive power of being in a group, each of us is drawn to believe that the group's value of the object is the true measure of its worth. Objects can have socially constructed value, even objects that have little intrinsic worth. This group valuation masks the object from view, as it were, and makes it difficult for anyone to distinguish its real, practical value.

This is, in fact, exactly what we have done with nuclear weapons. Beguiled by the apparent remarkable success of their first use at Hiroshima, we decided early on that they had enormous value. The rampant fear of the Cold War then made realistic reassessments threatening and difficult. Fear locked the groupthink in place and made reevaluation impossible.

This notion of nuclear weapons and their group-ascribed value comes from a remarkable essay by Anne Harrington de Santana that won the 2009 Doreen and Jim McElvany Nonproliferation Challenge, an international contest for the best essay about a topic connected with nuclear nonproliferation. In her essay, Harrington solved the puzzle of how nuclear weapons could be seen as so important for states even when the threat of their military use lacks all credibility.

Harrington argued that nuclear weapons are like currency. We live our lives (most of us) as if money were one of the most important things on the face of the earth. If you stop and think about it, however, the money itself has very little practical value. You can't eat it; you can't build a shelter out of it; it makes poor clothing.

Consider a man washed ashore on a desert island who is magically given a wish. He can have anything he wants. What should he wish for? A great stack of hundred-dollar bills, or a Swiss Army knife? A pile of gold coins, or fishhooks and some good nylon line? A credit card with a ten-thousand-dollar spending limit, or a pair of rabbits, one male and one female? On a desert island, money is worthless. It is only in a society that money has value.

The extent to which the value of money is socially constructed is illustrated by cowrie shells. Portuguese traders who explored the western coast of Africa in the 1400s discovered African tribes whose whole economy was based on cowrie shells.[3] Cowrie shells are small, rounded shells with openings that look like mouths with small teeth; they are found in tropical and subtropical oceans worldwide. But they were rare in the world of these African tribes. The Africans believed the shells had medical and religious powers. A bracelet or a necklace of cowrie shells could ward off sickness and protect the wearer from harm. A man with a large necklace of cowrie shells was a rich man. To West Africans, cowrie shells were money.

The Portuguese collected barrels of cowrie shells and brought them for trade to West Africa. They could not believe their luck. The Africans were willing to exchange *gold* for cowrie shells. The Portuguese were dumbstruck. These Africans traded worthless shells for the most valuable commodity in Europe. It was a chance for the sailors to make fortunes out of nothing. They must have laughed to themselves all the way back to Lisbon. "What a deal!" (or the Portuguese equivalent) they must have said.

But the Africans were laughing, too. They knew that gold was entirely useless. You couldn't eat it; it was unsuitable as clothing. You could build a house from it, but why would you want to? They had plenty of gold, more than they could ever use. In their lives, this dull yellow metal was common, and shells were rare. Shells were the most valuable thing in the world. And the Portuguese were willing to trade the most valuable thing in the world for a common, worthless metal. "What a deal!" they must have said.

Both of them, of course, were right. We instinctively think

the Portuguese were swindling the Africans because the military power of Europeans eventually brought (or imposed) their way of thinking to the entire world. But if the Africans had proved militarily unstoppable and had extended *their* monetary system around the world, we would all be shaking our heads at the silly Portuguese. This sort of excited exchange is what happens when two differing systems of value come in contact: things that are worthless in one economy can be priceless in another. Because of the human ability to imbue objects with value, different societies often value objects differently. These valuations can be (and usually are) largely independent of the actual usefulness of the object.

Currency is a medium of exchange. The physical object that you use as currency is essentially unimportant. It can be lumps of metal; it can be (as it was in ancient Rome) salt; or it can be pieces of paper with particular pictures and numbers on them. The actual object is, for the most part, beside the point. Any object that is durable and relatively rare can be used for currency.

And this is Harrington's central insight: nuclear weapons are tokens in a social exchange. They have become a currency of power. We use them to evaluate the strength of countries.[4] We use them to trade threats back and forth. We use them to judge which nations should be respected. It is often pointed out that the permanent members of the United Nations Security Council are all nuclear weapons states. The conclusion that most people draw from this is that a country needs to have nuclear weapons in order to be treated as a world power.

If nuclear weapons are tokens of power, like money, then it is not necessary for them to actually be useful in order to be sought after and valued. It is entirely possible for nuclear weapons to be relatively useless as military or political tools and yet still be avidly sought after as symbols of power.[5]

In fact, nuclear weapons make especially useful objects in a system of currency. Nuclear weapons have rarely been used; their practical value has been tested only once in war. It is especially easy, therefore, to construct their value and set it at any level that one wishes. When they are used, nuclear weapons are most often utilized as threats, which doesn't put their actual value to the test. Threats don't work by practical effects; they work by fear. People, unfortunately, are often afraid of things that are not sensible, practical, or even real. The bogeyman, for example, is a person (or perhaps a thing) used to threaten children when they misbehave. The bogeyman isn't in any way real, yet invoking his name often results in the desired outcome. Threatening children with an unknown (and unreal) danger has been effective for millennia. The fact that some nuclear threats appear to work does not prove anything about the actual effectiveness of the weapons. It is quite possible for nuclear deterrence to work for years even if nuclear weapons have no practical military value.

In a famous example in *Pragmatism*, William James pointed out that people don't check every fact for themselves. You see an object on the wall with hands and numbers and assume it is a clock; you don't open it up to check that it has the works of a clock inside.

> Truth lives, in fact, for the most part on a credit system. Our thoughts and beliefs "pass," so long as nothing challenges them, just as bank-notes pass so long as nobody refuses them. But this all points to direct face-to-face verifications somewhere, without which the fabric of truth collapses like a financial system with no cash-basis whatever. You accept my verification of one thing, I yours of another. We trade on each other's truth. But beliefs verified concretely by *somebody* are the posts of the whole superstructure.[6]

The problem with nuclear weapons is that there is no way to concretely verify the claims that are made about their importance. There is really only one data point — Hiroshima — determining their cash basis. The danger is that we have overinflated their value by misinterpreting that one event.

It seems to me that we don't really know what the value of nuclear weapons is. In pragmatic terms, no one is able to verify their special psychological power because they've been used only once. We have constructed an international system in which they are treated as if they are priceless, but as we've seen, this is no evidence that they are.

Reputation

Proponents might say, "All right, perhaps we've given nuclear weapons a little more than their due. Perhaps we've somehow mistaken their practical reality and ascribed more political power to them than they actually have. But given that we've made this mistake, given that they've become entrenched as the currency of power, shouldn't we accept the world the way it is? Nuclear weapons have this expanded reputation. The fear of nuclear weapons is real. It exists. The exaggeration is now the reality. Don't we have to deal with the reputation of nuclear weapons as it is?"

For the past thirty years many people have said that nuclear weapons are not actually intended to be used. Nuclear weapons' main function, their proponents say, is deterrence.[7] It can be argued, then, that it doesn't matter how many contradictions arise when one is contemplating their use. No one actually intends to use them. The important fact about nuclear weapons is not the practical consequences of their use in war. The real consideration is whether we can manipulate the fear they create. Many people argue that the crucial aspect to nuclear weapons is their *reputation* and the fear that that reputation engenders.

Perhaps the easiest way to understand why relying on reputation is so dangerous is to think about the story of Patroclus in the *Iliad*. Patroclus was Achilles's best friend, and together they joined the Achaeans in their war with Troy. At one point in the campaign, however, Agamemnon, leader of the Achaeans, insists that Achilles give up a beautiful girl name Briseis. Achilles has taken her as a prize in battle. Agamemnon now claims her. A violent quarrel erupts between Achilles and Agamemnon that stops just short of bloodshed. Achilles is forced to give up the girl and angrily swears that he will not fight again until his trophy is returned.

> *Someday, I swear, a yearning for Achilles will strike*
> *Achaea's sons and all your armies! But then, Atrides,*
> *harrowed as you will be, nothing you do can save you —*
> *not when your hordes of fighters drop and die,*
> *cut down by the hands of man-killing Hector!*[8]

Achilles is the greatest fighter among the Achaeans, and Homer tells us that without him, the tide of battle turns, and the Trojans drive the Achaeans before them: "they fled in panic. Back through stakes and across the trench they fled, and hordes were cut down at the Trojans' hands."[9]

Several people are sent to Achilles's tent to plead with him to rejoin the fighting before the Trojans win outright. But Achilles refuses to yield, and Achaean losses mount. Patroclus, Achilles's friend, comes to him and tries to reason with him. But not even Patroclus can mollify Achilles.[10] Finally, Patroclus says, If you won't fight, Achilles, can I at least borrow your armor and shield? Achilles assents. Patroclus takes the famous shield, shining breastplate, and helmet.

When Patroclus returns to the field of battle, the *reputation* of Achilles's armor does its work. The Trojans' reaction is predictable: "all their courage quaked, their columns buckled, thinking swift Achilles had [returned to the battlefield]."[11] For a while it looks as if Patroclus — using Achilles's armor — will win the day. The Trojans flee back to the shelter of their city's high walls. But Hector, son of King Priam of Troy and one of the Trojans' best fighters, is inspired by Apollo and returns to the field to challenge the man in Achilles's armor.

Led by Hector, the Trojans return to the fight. In the thick of things, the god Apollo steals up on Patroclus and knocks him down. Patroclus is not harmed, but his helmet comes off. The Trojans suddenly realize that it is not Achilles inside the famous armor; they surge toward Patroclus, and Hector drives a spear through him. "Death cut him short. The end closed in around him. Flying free of his limbs his soul went winging down to the House of Death."[12]

Patroclus relied on the reputation of Achilles to swing the battle in favor of the Achaeans. He wore the armor of Achilles and carried his shield as a way of using the fear of Achilles's military prowess to influence events. Unfortunately, reputation is not a very reliable means of defense. Accidents can undermine it. And there are always brave (or foolish) people who want to test the reputation of their opponents. Even if that reputation is fearsome.

Reputation is an empty suit of armor. We don't want the empty armor to protect us; we want the real warrior. We don't want Achilles's famous shield and breastplate to be our safeguard; we want Achilles himself. Real security can be achieved only when reputation is backed by actual capability. Relying on reputation alone can end with the false champion lying on the ground, his helmet off, spiked through with spears. It can be a prescription for disaster.

Because of the configuration of current nuclear arsenals, relying on their reputation is even more problematic. Even though the Cold War is long over, the United States and Russia keep large numbers of nuclear weapons on constant alert. Is it sensible to rely on a tremendously destructive, delicately balanced, hair-trigger system whose strength may be nothing more than perception?

Man-Made Problems

The fact that we have based so much of our thinking on myth and mistake is discouraging. But there is a lesson to be drawn from the attraction that the apocalypse myth has for us. At its heart, the apocalypse stories are about our lack of control over events. These stories tell us that our destinies, our hopes for survival, the fate of the entire world are in the hands of the gods. The apocalypse myth could be viewed as the ultimate expression of fatalism. It is a story in which *everything*, not just whether you get the promotion or your children outlive you, but *everything* — the very existence of the earth and all its peoples — is in the hands of the gods. When confronted with the possibility of apocalypse, it says, we can only bow our heads and accept our fate.

One could argue that the crucial move here, the reason that nuclear weapons have been incorporated into the apocalypse myth, is precisely so that we will feel helpless before them. Nuclear war will come "if the gods will it." When something is associated with apocalypse, the most important practical outcome of that incorporation — the action item, as it were — is that we no longer need concern ourselves with it. It is beyond your control.

There is no question that human existence demands humility. And there is a case to be made that humans are better off when animated by religious faith. There are larger forces in the universe that we are not in control of, and acknowledging that is simple realism. But there are strong reasons for believing that nuclear weapons should not be included in that list of forces beyond our control. To begin with, nuclear weapons are implements that we manage and use as we wish. If someone said, pointing to a hammer on the workbench, "That hammer is beyond our control," we would think that person was pretty peculiar. Why are we inclined to view nuclear weapons differently?

Nuclear weapons do seem to loom over us at times. They do make awe-inspiring explosions that seem to be on the same scale as forces of nature or acts of God. But these impressions do not give nuclear weapons volition. They do not magically give them independent life. The problem with imagining that nuclear weapons control our destiny, rather than the other way around, is that it encourages us to fall back on irresponsible inaction. It may be difficult to negotiate agreements to control nuclear weapons. But that does not make such agreements impossible or give us permission to throw our hands in the air and turn to other things. In a commencement address at American University in 1963 that has come to be known as the Peace Speech, President Kennedy talked about what the attitude toward difficult problems should be:

> First: Let us examine our attitude toward peace itself. Too many of us think it is impossible. Too many think it unreal. But that is a dangerous, defeatist belief. It leads to the conclusion that war is inevitable — that mankind is doomed — that we are gripped by forces we cannot control.
>
>   We need not accept that view. Our problems are man-made — therefore, they can be solved by man. And man can be as big as he wants. No problem of human destiny is beyond human beings. Man's reason and spirit have often solved the seemingly unsolvable — and we believe they can do it again.

Kennedy, of course, was expressing optimism about a much harder problem than the issue of nuclear weapons. He was talking about world peace. Taking concrete steps toward a world without war is far more formidable than coming up with sensible policies for nuclear weapons. But the central point that Kennedy was making applies to nuclear weapons: difficult problems have been solved in the past and they will undoubtedly be solved in the future. It is important to remain humble in the face of a complex and awesome universe. But there is no reason to believe that even the most difficult problems are insoluble.

CONCLUSION

I T TURNS OUT that much of what we thought we knew about nuclear weapons was based on myth. It's kind of scary to consider that all this time we've been making policy involving these deadly weapons using an intellectual structure that's based on wishful thinking. The principal thing we thought we knew — that they had a special power to overawe opponents — isn't true. The idea we built on that first impression — that they must be decisive in war — is open to doubt. The central idea of the entire field — that nuclear deterrence is robust and reliable — remains unproved. And the idea that nuclear weapons ensure peace just isn't supported by any reasonable standard of proof. The structure that we thought was built on top of good solid stones appears to have no foundation at all.

Nuclear Full Stop

Such radical changes in the foundations underlying nuclear weapons thinking might seem to call for equally radical changes in nuclear weapons policy. Indeed, some observers might argue that the deep and troubling questions raised here justify immediate abolition of nuclear weapons. But where so much is at stake, where the danger from a miscalculation is so great, caution is required. Sudden changes to a perilous status quo can lead to catastrophe. It would be foolish to act rashly, and in any event, a change in nuclear weapons policies will require the work of many hands—the cooperation of many nations. All of which will take time.

However, there are important steps that can and should be taken immediately. We need a nuclear pause: a period of reflection in which no new work is done on nuclear weapons. If the objections raised here prove to be sound, then serious questions are raised about the long-term viability of nuclear deterrence and the basic usefulness of nuclear weapons. Time is required to rethink nuclear weapons policies around the world. Just as a judge issues a stay forbidding work to go forward while a trial is held, so there should be a full-stop cessation of work on nuclear weapons.

Nuclear weapons need to be put on trial. This would not be the first time they've been brought up on charges. They have already been brought before the bench on a number of occasions. It's true they were acquitted every time, but this is different. New evidence has been submitted to the court, and new charges are being brought. This case will not be tried on morality and horror; this trial will be about practicality and usefulness. Nuclear weapons stand in the dock accused of being dangerous and nearly useless. It is a serious charge. Serious enough that while the trial is going on, there should be a pause in nuclear weapons activity.

A full stop has three elements. First, extraordinary efforts must be made to ensure that no new countries acquire nuclear weapons. The more nations that have nuclear weapons, the more likely nuclear deterrence is to fail. Second, nuclear-armed nations must halt any work on new weapons systems. If there are real questions about the usefulness of nuclear weapons, this is simple prudence. Third, spending on nuclear weapons should be reduced to maintenance levels. If the fundamental rationale for the weapons is in doubt, it makes no sense to spend new money until it's certain that the weapons will be kept.

And along with the pause, the safety of the world's leading nations has to be strengthened. This can be done only by deep reductions in U.S. and Russian arsenals. If nuclear deterrence can break down, if the shield that is supposedly keeping us safe is full of holes, then we need to decrease the possible effects of a catastrophic failure. To do that, it is essential to reduce the arsenals of the two largest nuclear-armed states to the low hundreds.

But the most important policy step is a fundamental rethinking. Government officials in all the nuclear countries (and other countries that would influence this issue) need to closely review nuclear weapons ideas and policies. The wisest scholars need to be enlisted to go back over the problem. Nuclear deterrence is clearly not as stable and secure as early theories asserted. Nuclear weapons are clearly not as useful as was originally claimed.

Such a rethinking has to address fundamental issues. How stable is nuclear deterrence? What does the latest neuroscience tell us about rationality (a necessary component of nuclear deterrence, but one that appears to be a less influential part of human makeup than we had thought)? Is there a real and sensible justification for keeping the weapons? Are there indispensable tasks that only nuclear weapons can accomplish? I have serious doubts that a positive answer can be given to any of these questions. Doubts about the usefulness of nuclear weapons only add weight to the admonition of George Shultz, William Perry, Sam Nunn, and Henry Kissinger that abolition should be our ultimate goal. A radical rethinking of policy may conclude that a swift and complete solution is both advisable and achievable. To find out, we must undertake the policy review.

Nuclear weapons pose an enormous danger. We have been living in far more danger than we knew. Sensible, prudent action is needed now.

Reality

The importance of totem poles is not that they are stumps of wood of a certain diameter and height that have been shaped with tools. Their significance is determined by what they stand for — by their place in a belief system. Belief and myth transform them from stump to totem.

The meaning is, as it were, an internal magic that quickens the stumps to life. Our minds and hearts pour this quicksilver into inanimate wood shapes and — magically — they are gods and heroes, demons and spirits.

It is a peculiar attribute of humans that we are able to infuse meaning into things. Meaning: noiseless, odorless, invisible, untouchable, but still the governor of what we perceive.

Much of the hold that nuclear weapons have on us is *psychological*. Their size in our mind's eye is not related to their size in the real world of pragmatic consequences. They are wrapped in a shroud of sixty years of rhetoric and hyperbole. We have attached such deep feelings to them that they have been transfigured. We constantly misconceive the problems and issues that are associated with nuclear weapons because we cannot see the weapons themselves with unblinking eyes.

It is a heretical notion in nuclear policy circles, but some of the most important work we face regarding nuclear weapons is emotional. We have to find ways to overcome the needs and desires that lead us to infuse them with meaning beyond their practical reality. That lead us to see nuclear weapons as either horsemen of the apocalypse or lightning bolts that give us the power of gods. We have to find the courage and honesty to see them plainly. Henry David Thoreau admonished us in *Walden*:

> Let us settle ourselves, and work and wedge our feet downward through the mud and slush of opinion, and prejudice, and tradition, and delusion, and appearance, . . . till we come to a hard bot-

tom and rocks in place, which we can call reality, and say, This is,
and no mistake; . . . Be it life or death, we crave only reality. If we
are really dying, let us hear the rattle in our throats and feel cold
in the extremities; if we are alive, let us go about our business.

What Next?

I am not certain what can or should be done with nuclear weapons. But I *am* certain that there must be a sweeping reevaluation
of nuclear deterrence and the study of nuclear weapons in general. The facts around Hiroshima should be closely reexamined.
The full history of the Cold War crises should be studied carefully
from end to end, with special attention paid to those episodes that
work against belief in nuclear deterrence. The efficacy of strategic
bombing and of killing civilians should be revisited and reargued.
The entire field, in other words, should be rethought using a close
attention to facts and pragmatism rather than myth and theory.

There's no question that nuclear weapons are dangerous. They
make escalation more likely and are likely to call forth an overwhelming desire for revenge. They spread poison in a swath for
hundreds of miles downwind, which almost assures that civilians
will be killed unnecessarily. Their size forces any use to be enormously destructive. At the same time, there are real doubts about
the value that we've assigned to nuclear weapons. Originally, policymakers assigned a value to them that was sky-high. Nuclear
weapons were the answer to every problem. Over time, that valuation has declined, but there is still no agreement on where exactly the value should be set. Are nuclear weapons indispensable
because they ensure nations' survival? Are they militarily decisive?
Or are they unusable even if you have a monopoly?

The story of nuclear weapons so far has been a tale of mistake
and exaggeration. We have been gripped by fear and made foolish
errors. We have transformed half-remembered events into mythic

truths that have almost no truth in them whatever. This is discouraging. But it is not all bad news. We have, after all, survived against the odds into the seventh decade of the nuclear era. We have not been called to pay for our mistakes with millions of innocent lives. We have the chance now to rethink the subject without the danger and almost unbearable pressure of the Cold War. We can break out of the deadlocked positions of the past.

When the story was originally told, nuclear weapons appeared in the role of the ultimate weapon. History was a long roll of technological developments that came to an end with nuclear weapons. No greater weapons would ever be invented. Indeed, human history itself might come to an end.

But in light of the facts reviewed here, nuclear weapons take on a different aspect. They begin to look less all-powerful. They seem to have real limits, particularly as deterrents. The fact that precision-guided munitions and small, stealthy drones have been increasingly used in recent wars but no appropriate use has been found for nuclear weapons since 1945 suggests we may have been fooled by their size. It may be that the biggest weapon is not the most useful one.

In the story of evolution, it wasn't the biggest beasts that ended up ruling the earth. The brontosaurus and *Tyrannosaurus rex* were awe-inspiring creatures. But they proved no match for changing circumstances and smaller, smarter, more adaptable species. Nuclear weapons are awe-inspiring weapons. But they seem equally unable to adapt. We may one day rewrite their story as the tale of an evolutionary dead end, a developmental experiment that in the end came to nothing. In some ways, this story already seems familiar. In the calm light of day, nuclear weapons seem like strange, abnormal weapons that never found a real role in the arsenals of the world.

The meaning of the story of nuclear weapons is that these weapons are not a looming danger that is set in stone. They are not some deadly fate we cannot escape. No sudden revolution in human nature is necessary to avoid a nuclear war. Nuclear weapons present a practical problem. They can be evaluated by normal measures of security and effectiveness. Because they are not a supernatural force but merely an ordinary, everyday problem, we can take sensible, prudent steps to deal with them. That is cause for hope.

ACKNOWLEDGMENTS

T HIS BOOK IS the result of a thirty-year journey, an intellectual odyssey that often took me for long periods of time far from the known world. I cannot list, much less thank, all the people I have been helped by or learned from. But let me at least mention a few.

First thanks go to David Hackett, who made me an RFK Fellow in 1981. David gave me permission to change the world and got me —somehow, without words—to believe I could. Gerard Piel comes next, who gave me a book contract to write a short, unbiased guide to nuclear weapons issues that left me stumped and confused. That failure, that inability to understand was essential. Joe Morris Doss stimulated my thinking and revived my spirit during the long days of our mutual exiles. Freeman Dyson befriended, taught, and encouraged me across twenty years and was the first person to see merit in the Hiroshima argument.

Michael Walzer was generous with his time and his unrivaled intelligence. Patricia Lewis invited me to participate in an important report for the Swiss government and has provided wise counsel since. (The smart things I've done were probably her idea; the dumb stuff I thought up on my own.) Tom Markram turned a chance conversation into a life-changing event. Jeffrey Lewis was generous with time and advice when I was unknown, as well as being relentlessly smart and wickedly funny. Barry Blechman gave me the opportunity to think about a world without nuclear weapons and other fundamental issues by commissioning me to write a chapter in his book *Elements of a Nuclear Disarmament Treaty*. Shivani Ray, my co-author on a paper that deepened my understanding of myths and their function in security debates, was a cheerful and invaluable ally.

I am grateful to the staff of Princeton University's Firestone Library, who fielded many requests over thirty years and guided me through corridors of invaluable scholarly resources. Zia Mian has been a steadfast source of encouragement and found me a job that allowed me to survive through a critical six-month period. Frank von Hippel arranged for me to be a Departmental Guest of the Program on Science and Global Security at Princeton University and has been a font of calm insight and analysis for nearly thirty years.

My agent, Martha Kaplan, is surely the best agent anywhere in the world: wise of counsel, generous with her time, steady in crisis, and deeply knowledgeable about the ways of the publishing world. My first editor, and the person who was willing to take a risk on this book, Amanda Cook, has my deepest gratitude. It takes a special kind of person to have the confidence to bet on the unknown. Bruce Nichols, who took up the project when Amanda left for other opportunities, is smart, worldly, and wise. Also thanks to Ben Hyman, Christina Mamangakis, Lisa Glover, and Ashley Gilliam for shepherding the book (and me) through the publication process.

There have been those who gave unrecompensed and generous financial support over the years. Bill and Lori let me live in their basement rent-free for a year. Ellen Gilbert was generous beyond any reasonable expectation. My parents were endlessly patient and helpful with my many and ongoing financial crises. Steffen Kongstadt saw merit in my work, and the Ministry of Foreign Affairs of Norway, which provides enormous amounts of money to causes great and small — including funding for writing this book — is responsible for much that is good in the world.

I am grateful to George Shultz, Henry Kissinger, William Perry, and Sam Nunn, whose courageous statements about the need for a world without nuclear weapons changed the entire context of the discussion and made it possible to get notions like the ones in this book into the mainstream of discussion.

My intellectual debts are many, profound, and difficult now to untangle. Freeman Dyson was an early and ongoing source of extraordinary sense as well as a model of what it is to think constructively outside of the accepted norms of a field. Dyson sent me to read P.M.S. Blackett, whose thinking is still, today, some of the most useful in the field. Bob Beisner taught me how to do history — its essentially human center, what sorts of questions and skepticism are necessary for the enterprise, and how much hard work is involved in doing it right. I am indebted, of course, to the large figures of the nuclear oeuvre, whose books I have read repeatedly and that even now I periodically go back to dip into: Bernard Brodie, Thomas Schelling, Herman Kahn, Robert McNamara, Robert Butow, Alain Enthoven, Lawrence Freedman, and others. Also important were Paul Boyer, Richard Betts, Marc Trachtenberg, Richard Ned Lebow, McGeorge Bundy, Alexander George, Richard Smoke, Richard Rhodes, and Jonathan Schell. There were also people whose work taught me things not about nuclear weapons directly but about the related, broader field of war: Theodore Dodge, A.J.P. Taylor, J. Glenn Gray, Robert O'Connell, Bruce Catton, Michael S. Sherry, Hannah Arendt, Geoffrey Blainey, Carl Maria von Clausewitz, B. H. Liddell Hart, Edward Luttwak, and Barbara Tuchman. William James and Ludwig Wittgenstein laid the pragmatic foundation that underlies much of what is here.

There are also others I have known in one way or another during otherwise solitary wandering whose memory I carry with me: Leslie, Margaret, Anna, and Ellen; John, Sara, Hannah, Daniell, Gordon, Frank, Jim; Nancy, Jean, and Betty; Arthur, Marion, Edmund, and Lillian; Richard, Ken; Brett, Emily, and Kori; Michele, Valerie, Christian, Fabian, the man who came and stood at the foot of my bed in a dream (and the man on the train), Paul, Nara, Benoit, Anne, Blair; Connie, Shel, Roger, Timothy, David, Tobias, Togzhan, Dionysus (in Pittsburgh), Bob, James, Hans, Michael, Marc, Rudyard, Alfred, Bruce, Denny, Arch, Eva, Jordi, Ludwig, Rob, Johan, Robert, W.B., Sarah, Brad, Ernest, William, John, Cormac, Russ, Nancy, Jackie, Linton, Cheryl, Contessa, Mohandes, and Martin.

Long journeys break or prove friendships. Bill, Kevin, and Rick, each in his own way, walked many of these miles with me. (And two of them, one time, fifty miles at once.) Bill, especially, my oldest and still best friend, has spent many, many hours of his life both arguing me into thinking more clearly in general and arguing me into sounder positions on this problem. His counsel, at different points, was critical.

My parents nourished me with love and each taught me lessons without which this volume would not have been possible.

In Matthew 20:16 it says that the last shall be first. And so it is here. My debt to the love, tenderness, courage, and staunch support of Lucill van Zyl is beyond repaying.

NOTES

Introduction

1. Harrington de Santana, "The Strategy of Non-Proliferation," 4.
2. Gaddis, "The Long Peace."
3. Dingman, "Atomic Diplomacy," 54.
4. George and Smoke, *Deterrence*, 135. For a somewhat different conclusion, see Betts, *Nuclear Blackmail*, 22–31.
5. Dingman, "Atomic Diplomacy," 54–55.
6. Perhaps this has something to do with the differences between the experiencing self and the remembering self described by Daniel Kahneman in *Thinking, Fast and Slow* (New York: Farrar, Straus and Giroux, 2011).
7. For a popular treatment, see Gottschall, *Storytelling Animal*.
8. Some of the most distinguished scholars have dismissed myths as nothing more than tall tales told by the unlearned. Even Sir James George Frazer, who wrote one of the seminal scholarly works on myths, *The Golden Bough*, was guilty of this error. See Ludwig Wittgenstein, "Remarks on Frazer's *Golden Bough*," in Lambek, *Reader in the Anthropology of Religion*, 79–81.
9. Clark, *Greatest Power on Earth*, 199.
10. Jungk, *Brighter Than a Thousand Suns*, 201.
11. This was, apparently, a rather flawed translation of the original text; Ramana, "Bomb of the Blue God."
12. This notion of nuclear war as apocalypse turned out to be a remarkably viral idea, considering there was no Internet to spread it. From the United States, the analogy swiftly traveled around the globe, and in each place it landed, it was immediately taken up and effortlessly became the conventional way to describe nuclear war. Here, for instance, is a conversation that took place in the 1980s between Dr. Eric Chivian, a

psychology professor at Harvard who advocates that the implications of nuclear conflicts be taught in schools, and Alla, a fourteen-year-old from Minsk (then in the Soviet Union, now in Belarus).

> Alla: If such an explosion were to happen somewhere, then for tens and hundreds of kilometers around the atomic particles will be distributed and everything will be destroyed. The planet will turn into a wasteland.
> Chivian: No animals?
> Alla: No.
> Chivian: Plants?
> Alla: Of course not. Everything will be diseased.
> Chivian: In the whole earth?
> Alla: Yes.

Eric Chivian, John Mack, and J. P. Waletzky, *What Soviet Children Are Saying About Nuclear Weapons* (Boston: International Physicians for the Prevention of Nuclear War Inc., 1983). This video was widely shown on national media, including ABC's *Nightline*, PBS's *MacNeil/Lehrer Report*, and NBC's *Today* show, among others. See also Eric Chivian et al., "American and Soviet Teenagers' Concerns About Nuclear War and the Future," *New England Journal of Medicine* 319, no. 7 (1988): 407–13.

13. See, for instance, sura 81.

> When the sun shall be darkened,
> when the stars shall be thrown down,
> when the mountains shall be set moving,
> . . .
> when heaven shall be stripped off,
> when Hell shall be set blazing,
> when Paradise shall be brought nigh,
> then shall a soul know what it has produced.

The Koran Interpreted, trans. A. J. Arberry (New York: Touchstone Books, 1955), 326.

14. For the Zoroastrian religion, see Pearson, *Brief History,* 20–23; for the Norse sagas, see ibid., 100–103.

15. Ibid., 90–91.

16. Ibid., 129–36. Pearson covers a number of other apocalyptic movements as well.

17. A long-lasting nuclear war is more than an idle possibility. See, for instance, Brodie, *Strategy in the Missile Age,* 160–64, in which he discusses the possibility of a "broken-backed" war. This would be a war in which the two sides traded devastating initial blows that left each of them un-

able to invade the other or impose an end to the fighting but neither of them sufficiently destroyed to quit the conflict. "The hope, so widely held between 1860 and 1914, that mechanized methods of warfare were making long wars an impossibility, has not been fulfilled. That hope was revived in 1945 when the first nuclear bomb was dropped on a Japanese city, but so far it has not been fulfilled. Even if two main nuclear powers went to war, the web of their alliances would probably turn it into a general war; and present knowledge offers no strong probability that a general war would be short. Even if it began with nuclear attacks there is no strong probability that it would end quickly. Although there seems a chance that a general war could end in a month, a disastrous month, there seems a greater chance that it would continue for years." Blainey, *Causes of War,* 227. Or, as he puts it succinctly on page 225, "General wars tend to be long wars."

18. "The development of the ideas of nuclear deterrence has reached an impasse. . . . Two views, locked in dialectic since the beginning of the thermonuclear age, appear at present as if imprisoned in amber." Bobbitt, *Democracy and Deterrence,* 3.

19. LeMay was the pugnacious and unapologetic commander of the air force units that mercilessly bombed Japan in the summer of 1945, and he was later one of the strongest advocates of nuclear weapons on the Joint Chiefs of Staff. LeMay and Kantor, *Mission with LeMay.*

20. Ludwig Wittgenstein, *Vermischte Bemerkungen,* quoted in Bobbitt, *Democracy and Deterrence,* vi.

21. Blainey, *Causes of War,* 55.

1. Myth 1: Nuclear Weapons Shock and Awe Opponents

1. Stimson, "Decision to Use," 105.

2. Ibid.

3. For example, Thomas Schelling recently described nuclear weapons as "weapons capable of coercing victory." Schelling, "World Without Nuclear Weapons?," 126.

4. Alperovitz, *Atomic Diplomacy.*

5. For views generally supporting the exhibit, see Martin Harwit, *An Exhibit Denied: Lobbying the History of the* Enola Gay (New York: Springer-Verlag, 1996), and Michael J. Hogan, "The *Enola Gay* Controversy: History, Memory, and the Politics of Presentation," in Hogan, *Hiroshima in History and Memory.* For criticism of the exhibit, see Robert P. Newman, "*Enola Gay* at Air and Space: Anonymity, Hypocrisy, Ignorance," in Maddox, *Hiroshima in History,* 171–89.

6. For the record, I happen to believe that the United States is a fundamentally good country. All countries make mistakes, and the United States has made its share, but I am proud to be a U.S. citizen.

7. Russian historians are an exception. They tell schoolchildren in Russia that the Russian declaration of war on August 9 is what caused Japan to surrender.

8. For traditional interpretations that accept that the Bomb was an important part of the Japanese decision to surrender, see Butow, *Japan's Decision;* Giovannitti and Freed, *Decision to Drop;* Feis, *Atomic Bomb and the End of World War II;* Sigal, *Fighting to a Finish;* Maddox, *Weapons for Victory;* Walker, *Prompt and Utter Destruction;* Newman, Enola Gay; and Bernstein, "Atomic Bombings Reconsidered." For the first suggestion that the Soviet intervention caused the Japanese surrender, see May, "United States, the Soviet Union."

9. *Seattle Post-Intelligencer,* August 15, 1945.

10. Some analysts have argued that the delay is understandable and cite historians' accounts that the Japanese government had failed to act decisively all summer long and that the vacillating emperor simply found it difficult to make decisions quickly. Drea, for example, in *Service of the Emperor,* page 215, characterizes the emperor as "a cautious procrastinator." However, on August 14, when leaflets were dropped on Japan that revealed to the public that secret surrender negotiations had been going on between the Japanese government and the Allies, Kido met with the emperor "within minutes" of seeing a leaflet, and Suzuki joined them shortly thereafter. They agreed to accept the Allied terms, and they moved up the time of the Supreme Council meeting from 1:00 P.M. to 11:00 A.M. The emperor and his advisers, therefore, were able to act swiftly in a crisis. See Frank, *Downfall,* 313–14, and Morgan, *Compellence,* 213–14.

11. Asada, "Shock of the Atomic Bomb," 506. Jungk says in *Brighter Than a Thousand Suns,* page 214, that the committee sent to investigate was still in Hiroshima on August 10.

12. Hasegawa, *Racing the Enemy,* 184.

13. Army deputy chief of staff Kawabe Torashiro also suspected that the weapon that destroyed Hiroshima might have been a nuclear weapon; see Asada, "Shock of the Atomic Bomb," 505–6. And the head of the operations division, Miyazaki, wrote in his diary on August 6 that "it may be the so-called atomic bomb." Quoted ibid., 505.

14. The Supreme Council often met quickly in response to events. For example, when the Allies issued the Potsdam Declaration, word reached Tokyo at 6:00 A.M. on July 27, 1945. They held a meeting to discuss it that day. The Supreme Council could meet on short notice in response

to an event; see Kirby, *War Against Japan,* 205. Also, despite numerous references to a meeting on August 7 to deal with Hiroshima, no such meeting was held. According to Foreign Minister Togo's testimony after the war, the meeting on the seventh was an ad hoc assembly of the ministers who were directly affected by the bombing: the minister of war, the minister of the navy, the minister of home affairs, and the minister of transportation; see Kort, *Columbia Guide to Hiroshima,* 388. Both Morgan and Asada assume that the meeting of the Supreme Council held on the ninth was the meeting that Togo had requested on the eighth. See Morgan, *Compellence,* 207, and Asada, "Shock of the Atomic Bomb," 488. However, the assumption that the meeting on August 9 was a delayed meeting that had been agreed to on August 8 is not supported by the evidence. See the discussion between Yonai and Takagi in which Yonai says that the meeting on the ninth will be about withdrawing troops from Burma (diary of Takagi Sokichi for Wednesday, August 8, 1945, quoted in Burr, "Atomic Bomb," doc. 55).

15. It is also telling that Togo was unable to get a meeting of the larger (and by now less important) cabinet to discuss Hiroshima. He apparently convened an emergency meeting of "key cabinet ministers" on the seventh, but because of army intransigence he was unable to get the full cabinet to take up his proposal. See Asada, "Shock of the Atomic Bomb," 486, and Kort, *Columbia Guide,* 388.

16. Historian Richard Frank, in the H-Diplo (diplomatic and international history discussion network) roundtable on Hasegawa's *Racing the Enemy,* argues that Japan's leaders would have discounted the Soviet invasion because they had already written off Manchuria and because the Soviet's paucity of amphibious landing craft made the possibility of an invasion of the home islands far less threatening than the sheer number of Soviet troops made it appear. This misses the point. The Japanese were not concerned about Manchuria. The Sixteenth Soviet Army, which was capturing the southern half of Sakhalin Island, had orders to be prepared to invade the home islands as soon as they had completed their mission. Frank's objection that the lack of landing craft would be fatal overlooks the fact that the Russians were making amphibious landings as part of the attack on Sakhalin Island and also in the attacks on all the Kuril Islands. Russia clearly had landing craft sufficient to invade Hokkaido. The strait separating Sakhalin Island from Hokkaido (the northernmost of Japan's home islands) is only twenty-one miles wide. Almost any craft would serve to carry the Soviet troops across. The Japanese troops defending Hokkaido (the Fifth Area Army) were understrength and had dug in on the east side of the island. The Soviet invasion was planned for the west side of the island. In addition,

the United States had a history of supplying crucial war materiel to the Soviets. Even presuming that the Japanese had accurate estimates of the numbers of Soviet landing craft (which is doubtful) and that they had confidence in those estimates, prudence would still have dictated that Japan's leaders assume the United States would supply their allies with the necessary invasion craft; see Thomas Maddux, ed., "H-Diplo Roundtable, *Racing the Enemy,* Roundtable Editor's Introduction," http://www .h-net.org/~diplo/roundtables/PDF/Maddux+HasegawaRoundtable .pdf.

17. For new research that has begun to question the role of the Bomb and emphasize the role of the Soviet Union (to a greater or lesser extent), see Dower, *Japan in War and Peace;* Pape, "Why Japan Surrendered"; Drea, *Service of the Emperor;* Asada, "Shock of the Atomic Bomb"; Frank, *Downfall;* Bix, *Hirohito;* Morgan, *Compellence;* and Hasegawa, *Racing the Enemy.* For a fascinating, in-depth discussion, see also Maddux, "H-Diplo Roundtable." A particularly detailed and useful summary of recent scholarship that also contains reproductions of many primary source documents is in Burr, "The Atomic Bomb."

18. Frank, *Downfall,* 253.

19. The strength of the Hiroshima bomb, which was originally estimated at 12.5 kilotons, has since been revised upward; see John S. Malik, *The Yields of Hiroshima and Nagasaki Nuclear Explosions* (Los Alamos, NM: Los Alamos National Laboratory, 1985).

20. Those who oppose nuclear weapons might question the use of the U.S. Strategic Bombing Survey casualty figures in order to measure the casualties of Hiroshima. There is, of course, dispute about the number of people killed at Hiroshima. All disasters engender debate about the extent of the damage and death. Since August 6, 1945, the number of people reported to have died at Hiroshima has steadily grown. Some people today quote casualty figures of 300,000 or more. This is preposterous, based on the facts. Rice rationing cards were distributed to everyone in the city, including recent refugees arriving from other areas. If you wanted to eat, you registered for a rice rationing card. There were 330,000 rice rationing cards given out in the first week of August. The mayor of Hiroshima, who was in a position to know, told authorities in Tokyo that one-third of the city's population was killed in the attack. This is roughly equal to the Strategic Bombing Survey's figure. There are, of course, reasons why one might believe this number should be higher. Some of these reasons seem relatively plausible. The problem is that where smart and creative people are involved, there are always plausible reasons for doing this or that. It is not possible to go back and recount the dead. My view is that, while in retrospect one might

plausibly see reasons to increase the estimated number of those killed, it is not permissible to change the historical facts to do so. Perhaps if new and compelling evidence appeared, one might consider adjusting the reported numbers. However, this new and better evidence has not been found. And there is another reason to doubt the increasing number of dead reported at Hiroshima. The number of deaths reported in historically important and emotionally charged events gets larger as time passes; this is a phenomenon familiar to historians. Over time, the casualty figures given for certain disasters tend to inflate. This is a simple-to-measure, quantifiable reality. It is true that sometimes initial casualty reports from a disaster are wrong for one reason or another. Authorities sometimes have a motive for undercounting the dead. But increasing the reported number of dead because one *feels sure* that more people must have died is not history. The killing at Hiroshima was horrible enough. There is no need to exaggerate. (See the discussion about casualties at Hiroshima in Frank, *Downfall*, 285–87.) It is sometimes argued that the undercount of the dead at Hiroshima resulted from not counting those who died from radiation. Because of the stigma of radiation poisoning, people were loath to admit that they were sick because of Hiroshima or Nagasaki; doctors didn't report them as dying of radiation poisoning; and the dead were therefore significantly underreported. This may be true. It certainly could not have had an impact on surrender debates, as most of the people who died from radiation poisoning died long after the surrender was an accomplished fact.

21. Comparisons between Hiroshima and conventional attacks seem inapt because of the higher casualty figures for the atomic attacks. But in order to demonstrate the helplessness of the military to protect Japan's civilians, the U.S. Army Air Forces dropped millions of leaflets announcing in advance some of the cities targeted for attack. As a result, many of the conventional attacks had far fewer casualties associated with them than would otherwise have been the case; see Bix, *Hirohito*, 495. Japan also developed effective systems for warning civilians of incoming bombers. The conventional attacks might have otherwise had much higher casualty rates than they did, which would have made them more similar to the two nuclear attacks. The night attack on Tokyo on March 9–10 inflicted enormous casualties, demonstrating how lethal conventional attacks could be.

22. Data for these figures comes from *United States Strategic Bombing Survey*, vol. 9 (New York: Garland, 1976), 42–43.

23. In fact, the question of whether the Japanese would be able to distinguish a nuclear attack from a large conventional raid came up during U.S. planning discussions. J. Robert Oppenheimer, who headed the sci-

entists trying to build the Bomb, responded that "the visual effect of an atomic bombing would be tremendous. It would be accompanied by a brilliant luminescence which would rise to a height of 10,000 to 20,000 feet." He went on to estimate that the Bomb would have the power of between two thousand and twenty thousand tons of TNT and would kill people by radiation for up to two-thirds of a mile. Read in light of the sometimes apocalyptic language used to describe nuclear weapons, Oppenheimer's answer seems curiously reserved. Quoted in Frank, *Downfall*, 256.

24. Brodie, *Strategy in the Missile Age*, 140.

25. Japanese officials initially speculated that the Americans might have suspended magnesium in the atmosphere prior to exploding the new device — that would have accounted for the very bright flash of light that witnesses spoke of; see ibid., 270.

26. Besides the bomber that dropped the bomb, there was another bomber taking photographs.

27. Bix, *Hirohito*, 491–92.

28. Asada, "Shock of the Atomic Bomb," 504.

29. Historian Richard Frank points out, "It is astonishing to note that these comments by Suzuki and one other isolated reference in May are the only documented references by a member of the Big Six to the strategic air campaign" (Big Six is another name for the Supreme Council); Frank, *Downfall*, 294n. Consider this comment from Admiral Toyoda during his postwar interview: "Q. In these conferences leading to the consideration of surrender, what value was put on the air assaults on JAPAN proper? How did they evaluate that when they were considering the matter of terminating war? A. I do not believe that the question of air raids came up in the minds of the members as an independent question at all; that is there was no idea that we must give up the war to avoid even a single additional day of bombing."

30. Cited in Morgan, *Compellence*, 216.

31. Quoted in Hasegawa, *Racing the Enemy*, 200.

32. For example, in the summer of 1936, while serving as attaché in Moscow, he sent several long cables advocating war with the Soviet Union; the idea had gained some currency in Japanese ruling circles, but Kawabe's advocacy was strikingly outspoken and aggressive.

33. Kort, *Columbia Guide*, 319.

34. Diary of Takagi Sokichi for Wednesday, August 8, 1945, quoted in Burr, "The Atomic Bomb."

35. These two were well placed to know what was going on in ruling circles: Yonai was on the Supreme Council, and Takagi was an admiral serving

as Yonai's secretary. Takagi was also part of a conspiracy of young officials in the government who were pushing to arrange surrender. See Bix, "Japan's Delayed Surrender," in Hogan, *Hiroshima in History and Memory*, 108.

36. Hasegawa, *Racing the Enemy*, 197.

37. Frank, *Downfall*, 289. See also Kort, *Columbia Guide*, 318.

38. Hasegawa, *Racing the Enemy*, 200–201. See also Kort, *Columbia Guide*, 311.

39. The various factions in Japan's government were not always forthcoming with information, particularly when it was bad news. Therefore, different groups within the government became aware of the invasion at different times. The military knew very shortly after the attack began; civilian leaders first heard about the attack at 4:00 A.M., when a Soviet radio broadcast was picked up by the foreign ministry. See Frank, *Downfall*, 288.

40. Interestingly, both the diplomatic and the military approaches were based on Japanese historical experience. Historians generally believe that Japan's experience in the Russo-Japanese War of 1904–1905 set the stage in many ways for Japan's plans and attitudes in World War II. The Russo-Japanese War consisted of a series of relatively inconclusive land campaigns, in which casualties were high, followed by a decisive naval battle at Tsushima Strait, which the Japanese dramatically won and which persuaded the Russians to seek an end to the war. This sequence of events was a clear parallel for the decisive-battle strategy that Japan's military leaders sought throughout World War II. Mediation also followed the model of the Russo-Japanese War, which was settled through the mediation of U.S. president Theodore Roosevelt. The war of 1904–1905 also began with Japan's surprise attack against its opponent's navy. For more on a decisive battle, see Drea, *Service of the Emperor*, especially chapter 12.

41. Quoted in Asada, "Shock of the Atomic Bomb," 504.

42. They were Kyoto (1,089,726), Nagasaki (272,000), Sapporo (206,103), Hakodate (203,862), Yokosuka (193,358), Kanazawa (186,297), Kokura (173,639), Otaru (164,282), Niigata (150,903), and Fuse (134,724). Figures are from the Japanese census of 1944. *Japan Statistical Yearbook* (Tokyo: Mainichi Shinbunsha, 1949), 42–43.

43. The three were Sapporo, Hakodate, and Otaru. *Japan Statistical Yearbook*, 42–43; and Kirby, *War Against Japan*, 165.

44. They were Kawaguchi (97,115), Asahikawa (87,514), Morioka (79,478), Akita (61,791), Urawa (59,671), and Takaoka (59,434). *Japan Statistical Yearbook*, 42–43. Asahikawa, Morioka, and Akita were out of range.

The thoroughness and extent of the U.S. Army Air Forces' campaign of city bombing can be gauged by the fact that they ran through so many of Japan's cities, they were reduced to bombing cities of thirty thousand or fewer people. In the modern world, thirty thousand people is no more than a large town. The student body of the University of Wisconsin at Madison would qualify — even without adding in the population of the city of Madison.

45. See Michael Walzer's wonderful and instructive essay about the responsibilities of leadership, "Political Action: The Problem of Dirty Hands."

46. It is noteworthy that more than one Japanese official referred to the Bomb as being heaven-sent: Yonai ("Heaven-sent blessings"), Sakomizu ("a golden opportunity given by Heaven"), and Suzuki ("an extremely favorable opportunity to commence peace talks").

47. Asada, "Shock of the Atomic Bomb," 484.

48. For a notable exception, see Ernest R. May, one of the most distinguished postwar historians in the United States. His article "The United States, the Soviet Union, and the Far Eastern War," published in 1955, argues — very gently — that the Soviet entry into the war was the key to Japan's surrender.

49. The Hatano quote is in Hasegawa, *End of the Pacific War*, 301; see Frank, *Downfall*, 291. All of these factors make it essential to rely on contemporaneous accounts in order to understand the decision to surrender. Minutes of meetings, actual documents from the time, letters, and diaries are not always foolproof renderings of the truth; diaries, for example, are sometimes written with an eye to the future. (For an illustration, see Kido's diary.) But in general, contemporaneous documents provide an invaluable window into the thinking of people at the time, the emotions and concerns of the moment. In evaluating the evidence about Japan's surrender, it is important to keep in mind the pressure on former government officials to shade the truth, and to give special weight to contemporaneous sources. Interestingly, historian J. Samuel Walker, in *Prompt and Utter Destruction*, pages 90–91, warned against taking postwar statements made by American officials too literally. Their judgment may have been affected, he said, "by bureaucratic interests, personal experiences, or even political ambitions." I think he is right. Ex post facto accounts often contain revisions of the actual events, either because the teller wants to come off better or because hindsight has reshaped what the teller believes he remembers.

50. Frank says, in connection with the August 7 meeting Kido Koichi had with the emperor at which they discussed Hiroshima, "This is the first of a series of incidents over the next tumultuous days where postwar evidence offered by Kido and others that places the Emperor in a favo-

rable light lacks contemporary confirmation in circumstances where it might be expected to exist." Frank, *Downfall,* 272.

51. Quoted ibid., 310.
52. Asada, "Shock of the Atomic Bomb," 507.
53. Kort, *Columbia Guide,* 361.
54. Quoted in Asada, "Shock of the Atomic Bomb," 567.
55. And if we look closely, we can even see evidence of the Bomb-as-face-saving-excuse during the surrender debate. In the crucial cabinet meeting on August 9, Tadaatsu Ishiguro, minister of agriculture and commerce, argued: "We have lost a scientific war. The people may be dissatisfied with the military for the defeat. But if we say we lost a scientific war, the people will understand." Quoted ibid., 507.

2. Myth 2: H-Bomb Quantum Leap

1. Gaddis et al., *Cold War Statesmen,* 35.
2. Churchill, *Hansard.*
3. Of course, the circle for a one-megaton bomb varies depending on the height of the blast and other factors. These numbers are only the roughest of approximations. The general point, however, that yield gives a false impression of the difference between bomb sizes still holds.
4. I asked the distinguished physicist Freeman Dyson to explain yield and destruction to me, and this is part of his reply. It gives a sense of the complexities involved. "The word 'destruction' is ambiguous, but it usually means the area of blast damage within which ordinary buildings are demolished. The destructiveness goes with the two-thirds power of the yield. For big yields in the megaton range, fire damage extends further than blast damage, and the destruction rises linearly with yield. For small yields in the sub-kiloton range, radiation kills more people than blast, and the destruction decreases more slowly than the two-thirds power of yield. The two-thirds power is valid roughly over the range between a kiloton and a megaton."
5. The actual size is classified, but this figure is drawn from conversations with people in a position to know and from general references in the public literature.
6. Freedman, *Evolution of Nuclear Strategy,* 93–94. "First, arguments on the efficacy of strategic bombing had been settled conclusively."
7. Brodie, *Strategy in the Missile Age,* 103.
8. Schelling, *Arms and Influence,* 17.
9. "The dramatic finale of World War II at Hiroshima and Nagasaki rescued the doctrine of strategic bombardment. Without the atom bomb the theorists of airpower would have been pushed on to the defensive,

hard put to justify the pounding of cities for limited rewards. With the atom bomb, airpower could be said to have come of age." Freedman, *Evolution of Nuclear Strategy*, 22.

10. Kahn, *On Escalation*, 134.

11. Although Euripides did not actually call for the abolition of slavery, he wrote plays that revolved around its cruelty (*Hecuba* and *The Trojan Women*), and he was probably exiled for these views. In *Hecuba*, the chorus says, "Alas, what an evil slavery has always been; It endures what is not right, overcome by force." See Stephen G. Daitz, "Concepts of Freedom and Slavery in Euripides' *Hecuba*," *Hermes* 99 (1971): 217–26.

12. See E. R. Dodds, *The Greeks and the Irrational* (Berkeley: University of California Press, 1951), especially chapter 6, "Rationalism and Reaction in the Classical Age."

13. U.S. strategists presumed that this lesson had been absorbed into Soviet military thinking. See, for example, Colin Gray, "Nuclear Strategy: A Case for a Theory of Victory," in Miller, *Strategy and Nuclear Deterrence*, 36.

3. Myth 3: Nuclear Deterrence Works in a Crisis

1. Glenn H. Snyder, "Deterrence and Defense," in Art and Waltz, *Use of Force*, 129; George and Smoke, *Deterrence*, 11; Schelling, *Arms and Influence*, 69.

2. Quoted in Rabe, "Cuban Missile Crisis Revisited," 59.

3. Kennedy, *Thirteen Days*, 23. Although see Scott and Smith, "Lessons of October."

4. Kennedy, *Thirteen Days*, 69–71.

5. Lebow, "Cuban Missile Crisis," 431.

6. Quinlan, *Thinking About Nuclear Weapons*, 27.

7. Scholars familiar with the Cuban missile crisis literature will likely conclude at this point that I am following in the footsteps of Barton Bernstein in criticizing Kennedy (see Bernstein, "Cuban Missile Crisis"), but I am emphatically not aiming to discredit Kennedy. John F. Kennedy is one of the presidents I admire most. I'm quite convinced that if I were in the same situation, if I had been lied to and stood to lose everything I had worked to accomplish, I would have behaved much less admirably than he did; my guess is that I would have launched the air strike with the full package of targets. Kennedy's behavior in the crisis was laudable. But I am interested in something more important than Kennedy's reputation in history: whether nuclear deterrence works. Failing to ask why Kennedy wasn't deterred because one happens to like Kennedy,

as I do, undermines any fair-minded investigation into the efficacy of nuclear deterrence.

8. "Text of Soviet Statement Saying That Any U.S. Attack on Cuba Would Mean War," *New York Times*, September 12, 1962.

9. Sorensen, *Kennedy*, 767.

10. Ibid., 795. McGeorge Bundy points out that Sorensen does not say that Kennedy's remark was about *nuclear* war, merely about war, which is true. However, it is difficult to imagine that a war fought in Cuba over nuclear missiles, with tactical nuclear weapons on hand and nuclear weapons aboard Soviet submarines near Cuba, would not have become a nuclear war. Bundy, *Danger and Survival*, 453. It is also true that one out of three and one out of two are not unbeatable odds. But given the catastrophic nature of a nuclear war, any risk is unacceptable.

11. See May and Zelikow, *Kennedy Tapes*. The possibility of nuclear war comes up frequently. In the first day alone, see the following: "eliminate the Cuban problem by actually eliminating the island," 54; "we'll be facing a situation that could well lead to general war," 56; "because I think the danger to this country in relation to the gain that would accrue would be excessive," 59; "he's the one that's playing at God, not us," 88; "Not the chances of success. It's the results that we're causing for mankind," 112. In addition, in the evening meeting on the first day, the ExComm members began to explore the possible ways in which such a crisis could escalate — in other words, they directly considered the risks of nuclear war. See the following: "It seems to me almost certain that any one of these forms of direct military action will lead to a Soviet military response of some type, some place in the world. It may well be worth the price," 87; "The second thing we ought to do, it seems to me, as a government, is to consider the consequences," 96; "this is why I think tonight we ought to put on paper the alternative plans and probable, possible consequences thereof," 99; "What happens beyond that. You go in there with a surprise attack. You put out all the missiles. This isn't the end. This is the *beginning*, I think. There's a whole hell of a lot of things," 115. Later in the crisis, in a discussion between the president and members of the Joint Chiefs of Staff, President Kennedy was even more explicit in painting the risk of nuclear war that the crisis created.

12. See, for example, James Nathan, "The Heyday of the New Strategy," in Nathan, *Cuban Missile Crisis Revisited*. Scott and Smith, in "Lessons of October," page 661, state: "In the United States there was a tendency to see nuclear superiority as vital in ensuring success in any future U.S.–Soviet crisis." There is a remarkable lack of historical knowledge displayed in some of these claims. The Kennedy administration had

a significantly different view of U.S. military superiority than we have now. They were working with intelligence estimates and best guesses, whereas researchers today are working from authenticated published numbers from Soviet archives. The administration tended to focus on numbers of missiles, because although bombers could get shot down, there was no effective defense against missiles. The United States had a large advantage over the Soviet Union in bombers, but in the crucial category of ICBMs (land-based missiles), the U.S. advantage was only 3.58 to 1. And McGeorge Bundy, the president's national security adviser, notes that at the time, the administration incorrectly believed that the Soviet Union had seventy-five ICBMs (rather than the fifty they actually had), which would have made the U.S. advantage only 2.39 to 1. The eight-to-one U.S. superiority that is used in some scholarly arguments about nuclear weapons was actually only a little better than a two-to-one advantage in Kennedy's estimation.

13. Blight, Nye, and Welch, "Cuban Missile Crisis Revisited," 177. A number of officials who advised the ExComm, including Roger Hilsman, Ray Cline, Raymond Garthoff, and Paul Nitze, also agreed to a greater or lesser extent. Roger Hilsman, who directed the State Department's Bureau of Intelligence and Research, gave half the credit to U.S. nuclear superiority, writing that "the Soviets backed down in the face of a threat that combined conventional and strategic power" (Hilsman, *To Move a Nation*, 227). Raymond Garthoff, of the State Department, while arguing that the "balance of resolve" played the most important role in the crisis and acknowledging the importance of U.S. conventional-weapon superiority, wrote, "Nevertheless, the strategic balance undoubtedly did persuade the Soviet leaders not to counter in some other situation where they had decisive conventional superiority, such as Berlin" (Garthoff, *Reflections*, 145–46). Paul Nitze, the principal author of NSC 68, a strong advocate of military strength, and the assistant secretary of defense for International Security Affairs, looked back after twenty-five years and said that the decisive factor during the Cuban missile crisis was "our undoubted nuclear superiority" (Blight and Welch, *On the Brink*, 147–48). Ray Cline, the head of the CIA's Directorate of Intelligence during the crisis and an adviser to the ExComm, said later that U.S. superiority made the chances of a nuclear war "no more than one in a thousand" (Cline, "Commentary," 191). And a number of people who were out of government agreed. Henry Kissinger, secretary of state under Presidents Nixon and Ford and at the time director of the Harvard Defense Studies program, wrote a month after the crisis that the "crisis could not have ended so quickly and decisively but for the fact that the United States can win a general war if it strikes first and can

inflict intolerable damage on the Soviet Union even if it is the victim of a surprise attack. . . . The credibility of our deterrent was greater than theirs" (Kissinger, "Reflections on Cuba," 21–24).

14. Blight, Nye, and Welch, "Cuban Missile Crisis Revisited," 174.

15. Most of the senior participants have denied that U.S. nuclear superiority mattered. They wrote in a retrospective article in 1982, "American nuclear superiority was not in our view a critical factor, for the fundamental and controlling reason that nuclear war, already in 1962, would have been an unexampled catastrophe for both sides." Rusk et al., "Essay." It is interesting to note that none of those who claim that nuclear superiority was a key factor were principals of the ExComm, while all of the officials signing this joint statement were. There is some evidence that this ex post facto statement matches the actual views of the participants at the time. McNamara, for example, asserted quite strongly that the missiles did not have an impact on the military balance in the first meeting on Tuesday, October 16, 1962. Theodore Sorensen submitted a memorandum two days after the missiles were discovered that argued, "These missiles, even when fully operational, do not significantly alter the balance of power" (see Sorensen, "Memorandum for the President."). It is also striking that the ExComm did not talk about nuclear superiority. While the risk of starting a nuclear war comes up again and again, the importance of U.S. nuclear superiority does not.

Kennedy himself left no definitive account of his views on the Cuban missile crisis. There are, however, two indirect pieces of evidence about his views. One aide reported: "The next morning he told me he was afraid that people would conclude from this experience that all we had to do in dealing with the Russians was to be tough and they would collapse. The Cuban missile crisis, he pointed out, had three distinctive features: it took place in an area where we enjoyed local conventional superiority, where the Soviet national security was not directly engaged and where the Russians lacked a case which they could plausibly sustain before the world" (Schlesinger, *A Thousand Days,* 759). Notably, Kennedy does not mention nuclear superiority.

Sorensen also noted that when Kennedy gave the moral of the story of the Cuban missile crisis in a speech at American University in 1963, it was not the importance of nuclear superiority (Sorensen, *Kennedy,* 782–83).

16. Bundy, *Danger and Survival,* 448. In the words of Garthoff, "A 'parity' of ability to retaliate in a devastating war was already in the hands of both the Soviet Union and the United States" (Garthoff, *Intelligence Assessment,* 24).

17. "The sensitive question of whether parity was giving way to Soviet

superiority thus depended on when one assumed parity had arrived, which in turn depended on which sort of parity one was talking about. If it meant mutual vulnerability to unacceptable damage, parity came in the mid-1950s; if it meant nearly equal levels of civil damage, it arrived by the early 1970s; if equality in missiles or delivery vehicles, by the mid-1970s; if the measure is the balance of forces as a whole or of counterforce capacity, by the late 1970s." Betts, *Nuclear Blackmail,* 188.

18. Historian Marc Trachtenberg has made an argument that places the fact that U.S. nuclear forces were put on alert during the crisis at its center. Trachtenberg argues that whatever one may think about the impact of U.S. superiority on U.S. actions, "the Soviets seem to have been profoundly affected by their 'strategic inferiority.'" He supports his argument with testimony that while the United States put its nuclear forces on alert, Soviet nuclear forces were not put on alert; see Trachtenberg, "Influence of Nuclear Weapons," 163. In the same article, on page 152, he quotes air force general David Burchinal talking about the Soviets having a gun to their heads. If that were true, this would be strong evidence of the impact of nuclear superiority on the crisis. Burchinal's evidence, however, seems doubtful from the outset. First, the scorn he feels for the Kennedy administration and his obvious anger about the handling of the crisis give him a strong motive for skewing the facts. Second, Burchinal reports events that cannot have occurred. In his description of a key moment in the crisis, Secretary of Defense McNamara turns white with fear and runs out of the room yelling, "The President must get the Russians on the hot line!" As a story, this is colorful as well as denigrating toward McNamara, but since the hot line between the United States and the Soviet Union was not put in place until *after* the Cuban missile crisis (in fact, it was installed *because of* the crisis), it cannot be factual. These issues undercut the value of Burchinal's testimony. More important, however, is that recent new evidence from the Russian side of the question apparently invalidates this argument. "Former Soviet officers with responsibilities for strategic nuclear forces have stated that the alert status of Soviet intercontinental ballistic missiles (ICBMs) and long-range nuclear bombers was increased from its routine peacetime status to the intermediate level, and then, for a brief period during the crisis, to the state of combat readiness, in which the nuclear warheads were mated to the missiles" (Scott and Smith, "Lessons of October," 672).

19. Trachtenberg, "Influence of Nuclear Weapons," 147.

20. Dobbs, *One Minute to Midnight,* 254–75.

21. Ibid., 297–303 and 317–18.
22. Ibid., 230–37 and 241–42.
23. Ibid., 124–25, 205–6, 248–50, and 351–52.
24. See http://www.jfklibrary.org/Research/Ready-Reference/JFK
    -Speeches/Commencement-Address-at-American-University-June
    -10-1963.aspx.
25. See, for example, Gaddis, *The Long Peace.*
26. Typical of historians' treatment of this crisis is John Lewis Gaddis's han-
    dling of the event. Gaddis emphasizes the implicit threat delivered by
    redeploying B-29s to Great Britain and completely ignores the issue of
    how the Soviets could have been so unimpressed with the U.S. nuclear
    monopoly that they would initiate the events that led to the crisis. Gad-
    dis asserts that the threat worked by redefining the goal of the threat,
    and he does this without, as far as I can tell, any evidence. Gaddis claims
    that the point of the redeployment was not the obvious one of lifting the
    Berlin blockade. The redeployment's objective, he says, "was to keep
    the Russians from interfering with the Berlin airlift" (Gaddis, *The Long
    Peace,* 110). If the threat's objective was to lift the Berlin blockade (a
    reasonable supposition), then it could hardly be said to have worked
    decisively: the blockade continued for almost another six months. But
    by moving the goalposts and making the redeployment's objective to
    prevent interference with the airlift, Gaddis redefines the threat as a
    success.
27. Gaddis, *The Long Peace,* 120–21 and 110. See also Dingman, "Atomic
    Diplomacy," 54–55.
28. Again, see Gaddis, *The Long Peace,* for the orthodox treatment of this
    nuclear threat. Although Gaddis makes much of the redeployment of
    bombers to Great Britain during the Berlin blockade, he neglects to
    mention the redeployment of B-29s in the Pacific that failed to prevent
    the Chinese from declaring and fighting a war against U.S. forces. See
    chapter 5, "The Origins of Self-Deterrence," 104–46. Again, deterrence
    "successes" are prominently discussed. Failures are walked by in silence.
29. See, for example, Barry M. Blechman and Douglas M. Hart, "The Politi-
    cal Utility of Nuclear Weapons: The 1973 Middle East Crisis," in Lebow
    and Stein, *We All Lost the Cold War.*
30. Chilton and Weaver, "Waging Deterrence."
31. Lebow, "Cuban Missile Crisis," 457. Michael Quinlan agreed, writing,
    "Libraries-full of writing have accumulated about deterrence theory
    centred upon nuclear weapons" (Quinlan, *Thinking About Nuclear
    Weapons,* 20).
32. Lebow, "Cuban Missile Crisis," 457.

33. "When deterrence 'fails,' analysts do not blame the theory, but the policymakers who attempted to implement it — somehow they did not succeed in imparting sufficient credibility to their commitment. Perhaps this explains what has happened with regard to the Cuban missile crisis. Analysts, working within the dominant paradigm, have gone to great lengths to make the case consistent with the theory. As a result, the paradigm has drawn their attention away from what may be a more interesting and important question about the crisis" (ibid.).

34. I am indebted to Dr. Patricia Lewis for bringing this argument to my attention.

4. Myth 4: Nuclear Weapons Keep Us Safe

1. Gaddis, "The Long Peace"; Gaddis, *The Long Peace*.
2. Gaddis, *The Long Peace*, 232.
3. See, for instance, Tertrais, "In Defense of Deterrence."
4. For example, the British general Rupert Smith believes that "industrial war no longer exists" and attributes the change to the introduction of nuclear weapons (see Smith, *The Utility of Force*, 4).
5. For a more factual account of actual volcano worship (including volcano worship involving human sacrifice), see David K. Chester and Angus M. Duncan, "Geomythology, Theodicy, and the Continuing Relevance of Religious Worldviews on Responses to Volcanic Eruptions," in Grattan and Torrence, *Living Under the Shadow*, 203–20, especially table 10.1 on page 206.
6. Pinker, *Better Angels*, xxii.
7. Ibid.; see, for instance, the list of deaths on page 195 and the associated graph on page 197.
8. Ibid., 189–94.
9. Blainey, *Causes of War*, 206.
10. Historian Ulric Nef, quoted ibid., 14.
11. Ibid., 30.
12. Ibid., 24.
13. Tertrais, "Correspondence," *Nonproliferation Review* 16, no. 2 (July 2009): 133
14. Smith, *Utility of Force*, 4.
15. Blainey, *Causes of War*, 29–30.
16. For a useful introduction to the issues around the origins of war, see Bramson and Goethals, *War*.
17. Kennedy, *To Seek a Newer World*, 149–50. Reprinted courtesy of the Robert F. Kennedy Center for Justice & Human Rights.

5. Myth 5: There Is No Alternative

1. In books (for instance, Stansfield, *Caging the Nuclear Genie*), articles, and op-eds too numerous to count.

2. There are, of course, analogies from history. Cortés, for example, was successful in part because the Aztecs believed that the gunpowder weapons the Spaniards used were magic. See O'Connell, *Of Arms and Men*, 128.

3. Although Harrington mentions trade between Portuguese traders and Africans, this example is mine. Harrington cites an author who actually disputes the historicity of this encounter, though others do not.

4. Geoffrey Blainey argues that the value of political things is more difficult to fix than the value of things in a real market. "The diplomatic market however is not as sophisticated as the mercantile market. Political currency is not so easily measured as economic currency. Buying and selling in the diplomatic market is much closer to barter, and so resembles an ancient bazaar in which the traders have no accepted medium of exchange." Blainey, *Causes of War*, 115.

5. Harrington and I disagree here. She emphasizes that the power of nuclear weapons is not symbolic but real. I'm inclined to think that they are symbolic. To understand the dispute, read her essay.

6. James, *Writings*, 576–77.

7. Colin Gray characterized the debate this way in the summer of 1979: "By definition it is assumed that nuclear war cannot be waged intelligently for rational political ends: the overriding function of nuclear weapons is the deterrence, not the waging of war." See Colin Gray, "Nuclear Strategy: The Case for a Theory of Victory," in Miller, *Strategy and Nuclear Deterrence*, 31–32.

8. Homer, *Iliad*, 85. Atrides is another name used for Agamemnon.

9. Ibid., 242.

10. For an excellent account of the meaning of the *Iliad*, see Caroline Alexander, *The War That Killed Achilles* (New York: Viking, 2006).

11. Homer, *Iliad*, 421.

12. Ibid., 440.

BIBLIOGRAPHY

This bibliography was assembled working outside the standard schools of thought about nuclear weapons. It may, as a result, be somewhat idiosyncratic.

Abraham, Itty. *The Making of the Indian Atomic Bomb: Science, Secrecy, and the Postcolonial State.* New York: Zed Books, 1998.

Abrahms, Max. "Why Terrorism Does Not Work." *International Security* 31, no. 2 (2006): 42–78.

Ackland, Len, and Steven McGuire, eds. *Assessing the Nuclear Age.* Chicago: Educational Foundation for Nuclear Science, 1986.

Adams, Gordon. *The Iron Triangle: The Politics of Defense Contracting.* New York: Council on Economic Priorities, 1981.

Adams, Ruth, and Susan Cullen, eds. *The Final Epidemic: Physicians and Scientists on Nuclear War.* Chicago: Educational Foundation for Nuclear Science, 1981.

Addison, Paul, and Jeremy A. Crang, eds. *Firestorm: The Bombing of Dresden, 1945.* Chicago: Ivan R. Dee, 2006.

Aldridge, Robert C. *The Counterforce Syndrome: A Guide to U.S. Nuclear Weapons and Strategic Doctrine.* Washington, DC: Transnational Institute, 1978.

Alexander, John B. *Future War: Non-Lethal Weapons in Twenty-First-Century Warfare.* New York: St. Martin's Press, 1999.

Allison, Graham T. *Essence of Decision: Explaining the Cuban Missile Crisis.* Boston: Little, Brown, 1971.

Allyn, Bruce J., James G. Blight, and David A. Welch. "Essence of Revision:

Moscow, Havana, and the Cuban Missile Crisis." *International Security* 14, no. 3 (1989): 136–72.

Alperovitz, Gar. *Atomic Diplomacy: Hiroshima and Potsdam*. New York: Simon and Schuster, 1965.

———. "Hiroshima: Historians Reassess." *Foreign Policy* 99 (1995): 15–34.

Alperovitz, Gar, and Sanho Tree. *The Decision to Use the Atomic Bomb and the Architecture of an American Myth*. New York: Alfred A. Knopf, 1995.

Andrews, Valerie, Robert Bosnak, and Karen Walter Goodwin, eds. *Facing Apocalypse*. Dallas: Spring Publications, 1987.

Arendt, Hannah. *On Violence*. New York: Harcourt, Brace and World, 1969.

Arkin, William M. "Calculated Ambiguity: Nuclear Weapons and the Gulf War." *Washington Quarterly* 19, no. 4 (1996): 3–16.

Aron, Raymond. *The Century of Total War*. Garden City, NY: Doubleday, 1954.

———. *The Great Debate: Theories of Nuclear Strategy*. Garden City, NY: Doubleday, 1965.

———. *On War*. Garden City, NY: Doubleday, 1959.

Art, Robert J., and Robert Jervis. *International Politics: Anarchy, Force, Political Economy, and Decision Making*. Boston: Little, Brown, 1985.

Art, Robert J., and Kenneth N. Waltz, eds. *The Use of Force: Military Power and International Politics*. New York: University Press of America, 1983.

Asada, Sadao. "The Shock of the Atomic Bomb and Japan's Decision to Surrender: A Reconsideration." *Pacific Historical Review* 67, no. 4 (1998): 477–512.

Axinn, Sidney. *A Moral Military*. Philadelphia: Temple University Press, 1989.

Bacevich, Andrew J. *The New American Militarism: How Americans Are Seduced by War*. New York: Oxford University Press, 2005.

Badash, Lawrence. *A Nuclear Winter's Tale: Science and Politics in the 1980s*. Cambridge, MA: MIT Press, 2009.

Baker, Nicholson. *Human Smoke: The Beginnings of World War II, the End of Civilization*. New York: Simon and Schuster, 2008.

Ball, Desmond, and Jeffrey Richelson, eds. *Strategic Nuclear Targeting*. Ithaca, NY: Cornell University Press, 1986.

Bandelier, Adolph F. "Traditions of Pre-Columbian Earthquakes and Volcanic Eruptions in Western South America." *American Anthropologist* 8, no. 1 (1906): 47–81.

Barker, Elisabeth. "The Berlin Crisis, 1958–1962." *International Affairs* 39, no. 1 (1963): 59–73.

Barnet, Richard J. *Real Security: Restoring American Power in a Dangerous Decade*. New York: Simon and Schuster, 1981.

Barnet, Richard J., and Richard A. Falk, eds. *Security in Disarmament.* Princeton, NJ: Princeton University Press, 1965.

Baumgartner, Frederic J. *Longing for the End: A History of Millennialism in Western Civilization.* New York: Palgrave, 1999.

Baylis, John, and John Garnett, eds. *Makers of Nuclear Strategy.* New York: St. Martin's Press, 1991.

Beitz, Charles R., Marshall Cohen, Thomas Scanlon, and John A. Simmons, eds. *International Ethics.* Princeton, NJ: Princeton University Press, 1990.

Benedict, Ruth. *The Chrysanthemum and the Sword: Patterns of Japanese Culture.* New York: Mariner Books, 2005.

Beres, Louis René. *Apocalypse: Nuclear Catastrophe in World Politics.* Chicago: University of Chicago Press, 1980.

Bernstein, Barton J. "The Atomic Bombings Reconsidered." *Foreign Affairs* 74, no. 1 (1995): 135–52.

———. "Book Review of *The Cuban Missile Crisis of 1962: Needless or Necessary?,* by William J. Medland." *Journal of American History* 76, no. 3 (December 1989): 992–93.

———. "The Cuban Missile Crisis: Trading the Jupiters in Turkey?" *Political Science Quarterly* 95, no. 1 (Spring 1980): 97–125.

———. "Why We Didn't Use Poison Gas in World War II." *American Heritage* 36, no. 5 (August/September 1985): 40–45.

Betts, Richard K. *Conflict After the Cold War.* Boston: Allyn and Bacon, 1994.

———. *Nuclear Blackmail and Nuclear Balance.* Washington, DC: Brookings Institution, 1987.

———. "A Nuclear Golden Age?: The Balance Before Parity." *International Security* 11, no. 3 (1986): 3–32.

Bird, Kai, and Lawrence Lifschultz. *Hiroshima's Shadow.* Stony Creek, CT: Pamphleteer's Press, 1998.

Bix, Herbert P. *Hirohito and the Making of Modern Japan.* New York: HarperCollins, 2000.

———. "Japan's Surrender Decision and the Monarchy: Staying the Course in an Unwinnable War." Posted on JapanFocus.org, July 5, 2005.

Black, Jeremy. *War in the New Century.* New York: Continuum, 2001.

Black, Samuel. *The Changing Political Utility of Nuclear Weapons: Nuclear Threats from 1970 to 2010.* Washington, DC: Henry L. Stimson Center, 2010.

Blackaby, Frank, Jozef Goldblat, and Sverre Lodgaard, eds. *No-First-Use.* Philadelphia: Taylor and Francis, 1984.

Blackaby, Frank, and Tom Milne, eds. *A Nuclear-Weapon-Free World: Steps Along the Way.* New York: St. Martin's Press, 2000.

Blacker, Coit D. *Reluctant Warriors: The United States, the Soviet Union, and Arms Control*. New York: W. H. Freeman, 1987.

Blackett, P.M.S. *Atomic Weapons and East-West Relations*. London: Cambridge University Press, 1956.

———. *Studies of War*. New York: Hill and Wang, 1962.

Blainey, Geoffrey. *The Causes of War*. New York: Free Press, 1973.

Blake, Nigel, and Kay Pole, eds. *Objections to Defence: Philosophers on Deterrence*. London: Routledge and Kegan Paul, 1984.

Blechman, Barry M., and Alexander K. Bollfrass, eds. *Elements of a Nuclear Disarmament Treaty*. Washington, DC: Henry L. Stimson Center, 2010.

Blechman, Barry M., and Cathleen S. Fisher. "Phase Out the Bomb." *Foreign Policy* 97 (Winter 1994/1995): 79–96.

Blight, James G. "How Might Psychology Contribute to Reducing the Risk of Nuclear War?" *Political Psychology* 7, no. 4 (1986): 617–60.

Blight, James G., Joseph S. Nye Jr., and David A. Welch. "The Cuban Missile Crisis Revisited." *Foreign Affairs* 66, no. 1 (1987): 170–88.

Blight, James G., and David A. Welch. *On the Brink: Americans and Soviets Reexamine the Cuban Missile Crisis*. New York: Hill and Wang, 1989.

Bobbitt, Philip. *Democracy and Deterrence: The History and Future of Nuclear Strategy*. New York: St. Martin's Press, 1988.

———. *The Shield of Achilles: War, Peace, and the Course of History*. New York: Alfred A. Knopf, 2002.

Bobbitt, Philip, Lawrence Freedman, and Gregory F. Treverton, eds. *U.S. Nuclear Strategy: A Reader*. New York: New York University Press, 1989.

Bonney, Richard. *The Thirty Years' War, 1618–1648*. Long Island City, NY: Osprey, 2002.

Boot, Max. *War Made New: Technology, Warfare, and the Course of History, 1500 to Today*. New York: Gotham Books, 2006.

Borrie, John. *Unacceptable Harm: A History of How the Treaty to Ban Cluster Munitions Was Won*. New York: United Nations Publications, 2009.

Borrie, John, and Ashley Thornton. *The Value of Diversity in Multilateral Disarmament Work*. New York: UNIDIR, 2008.

Boston Study Group. *Winding Down: The Price of Defense*. New York: Times Books, 1979.

Bourke, Joanna. *An Intimate History of Killing: Face-to-Face Killing in Twentieth-Century Warfare*. London: Granta, 1999.

Bousquet, Antoine. *The Scientific Way of Warfare: Order and Chaos on the Battlefields of Modernity*. New York: Columbia University Press, 2009.

Boyer, Paul. *By the Bomb's Early Light: American Thought and Culture at the Dawn of the Atomic Age*. New York: Pantheon, 1985.

Boyle, Francis A. *The Criminality of Nuclear Deterrence: Could the U.S. War on Terrorism Go Nuclear?* Atlanta: Clarity Press, 2002.

Bracken, Paul. *The Command and Control of Nuclear Forces.* New Haven, CT: Yale University Press, 1983.

Bramson, Leon, and George Goethals, eds. *War: Studies from Psychology, Sociology, Anthropology.* New York: Basic Books, 1968.

Broad, William J. *Star Warriors: A Penetrating Look into the Lives of the Young Scientists Behind Our Space Age Weaponry.* New York: Simon and Schuster, 1985.

Brodie, Bernard. *Strategy in the Missile Age.* Princeton, NJ: Princeton University Press, 1971.

Brooks, Lester. *Behind Japan's Surrender: The Secret Struggle That Ended an Empire.* Stamford, CT: De Gustibus Press, 1968.

Brown, Andrew, and Lorna Arnold. "The Quirks of Nuclear Deterrence." *International Relations* 24, no. 3 (2010): 293–312.

Brown, Michael E., Owen R. Coté Jr., Sean M. Lynn-Jones, and Steven E. Miller, eds. *Going Nuclear: Nuclear Proliferation and International Security in the Twenty-First Century.* Cambridge, MA: MIT Press, 2010.

——. *Offense, Defense, and War.* Cambridge, MA: MIT Press, 2004.

——. *Rational Choice and Security Studies: Stephen Walt and His Critics.* Cambridge, MA: MIT Press, 2000.

——. *Theories of War and Peace.* Cambridge, MA: MIT Press, 1999.

Brown, Seyom. *The Causes and Prevention of War.* New York: St. Martin's Press, 1987.

Brune, Lester H. *The Missile Crisis of October 1962: A Review of Issues and References.* Claremont, CA: Regina Books, 1985.

Bundy, McGeorge. *Danger and Survival: Choices About the Bomb in the First Fifty Years.* New York: Random House, 1988.

Bundy, McGeorge, William J. Crowe, and Sidney D. Drell. *Reducing Nuclear Danger: The Road Away from the Brink.* New York: Council on Foreign Relations, 1993.

Bundy, William P., ed. *The Nuclear Controversy.* New York: Signet, 1981.

Bunge, William. *Nuclear War Atlas.* New York: Basil Blackwell, 1988.

Bunn, George, and Christopher Chyba, eds. *U.S. Nuclear Weapons Policy: Confronting Today's Threats.* Washington, DC: Brookings Institution, 2006.

Bunn, Matthew, and Anthony Wier. "The Seven Myths of Nuclear Terrorism." *Current History* 104, no. 681 (2005): 153–61.

Burns, Richard Dean. *The Evolution of Arms Control: From Antiquity to the Nuclear Age.* Santa Barbara, CA: ABC-CLIO, 2009.

Burr, William, ed. "The Atomic Bomb and the End of World War II: A Collection of Primary Sources." National Security Archive Electronic Briefing Book no. 162, National Security Archive, August 5, 2005, http://www.gwu.edu/~nsarchiv/NSAEBB/NSAEBB162/index.htm.

Buruma, Ian. "Ecstatic About Pearl Harbor." *New York Review of Books*, October 14, 2010.

Butow, Robert J. C. *Japan's Decision to Surrender.* Stanford, CA: Stanford University Press, 1954.

Caldicott, Helen. *Nuclear Madness.* New York: Bantam Books, 1980.

Canaday, John. *The Nuclear Muse: Literature, Physics, and the First Atomic Bombs.* Madison: University of Wisconsin Press, 2000.

Carnesale, Albert, Paul Doty, Stanley Hoffmann, Samuel P. Huntington, Joseph S. Nye Jr., and Scott D. Sagan. *Living with Nuclear Weapons.* New York: Bantam Books, 1983.

Carr, Caleb. *The Lessons of Terror: A History of Warfare Against Civilians.* New York: Random House, 2003.

Carroll, James. *House of War: The Pentagon and the Disastrous Rise of American Power.* Boston: Houghton Mifflin, 2006.

Carter, Ashton B., and David N. Schwartz, eds. *Ballistic Missile Defense.* Washington, DC: Brookings Institution, 1984.

Caspary, William R. "New Psychoanalytic Perspectives on the Causes of War." *Political Psychology* 14, no. 3 (1993): 417–46.

Casson, Lionel. *Ships and Seamanship in the Ancient World.* Princeton, NJ: Princeton University Press, 1971.

Chang, Gordon G. *Nuclear Showdown: North Korea Takes on the World.* New York: Random House, 2006.

Chang, Laurence, and Peter Kornbluh, eds. *The Cuban Missile Crisis, 1962: A National Security Archive Documents Reader.* Rev. ed. New York: New Press, 1998.

Chernus, Ira. *Dr. Strangegod: On the Symbolic Meaning of Nuclear Weapons.* Columbia: University of South Carolina Press, 1986.

———. "Mythologies of Nuclear War." *Journal of the American Academy of Religion* 50, no. 2 (1982): 255–73.

Chilton, Kevin, and Greg Weaver. "Waging Deterrence in the Twenty-First Century." *Strategic Studies Quarterly* (2009): 31–42.

Chirot, Daniel, and Clark McCauley. *Why Not Kill Them All?: The Logic and Prevention of Mass Political Murder.* Princeton, NJ: Princeton University Press, 2006.

Chivian, Eric, Susanna Chivian, Robert Jay Lifton, and John E. Mack, eds. *Last Aid: The Medical Dimensions of Nuclear War.* San Francisco: W. H. Freeman, 1982.

Churchill, Winston. *Hansard* (Commons), 5th series, vol. 537, col. 1899, March 1, 1955.

Cirincione, Joseph. *Bomb Scare: The History and Future of Nuclear Weapons.* New York: Columbia University Press, 2007.

Clark, Ian. *Limited Nuclear War*. Princeton, NJ: Princeton University Press, 1982.

Clark, Ronald W. *The Greatest Power on Earth: The International Race for Nuclear Supremacy*. New York: Harper and Row, 1980.

Clausewitz, Carl von. *Historical and Political Writings*. Translated by Peter Paret and Daniel Moran. Princeton, NJ: Princeton University Press, 1992.

——. *On War*. London: Penguin Books, 1968.

——. *On War*. Translated by Michael Howard and Peter Paret. Princeton, NJ: Princeton University Press, 1976.

——. *War, Politics, and Power*. Translated by Edward M. Collins. Washington, DC: Regnery Gateway, 1962.

Cline, Ray S. "Commentary: The Cuban Missile Crisis." *Foreign Affairs* 68, no. 4 (Fall 1989): 190–96.

Clodfelter, Mark. *The Limits of Air Power: The American Bombing of North Vietnam*. New York: Free Press, 1989.

Cobban, Helena. *Amnesty After Atrocity?* Boulder, CO: Paradigm, 2007.

Cockburn, Andrew. *The Threat: Inside the Soviet Military Machine*. New York: Random House, 1983.

Cohen, Avner. "The Last Taboo: Israel and the Bomb." *Current History* 104, no. 681 (2005): 169–75.

Cohen, Avner, and Steven Lee, eds. *Nuclear Weapons and the Future of Humanity: The Fundamental Questions*. Totowa, NJ: Rowman and Littlefield, 1986.

Cohen, Marshall, Thomas Nagel, and Thomas Scanlon, eds. *War and Moral Responsibility: A Philosophy and Public Affairs Reader*. Princeton, NJ: Princeton University Press, 1974.

Cohen, Raymond. *Threat Perception in International Crisis*. Madison: University of Wisconsin Press, 1979.

Cohn, Carol. "Sex and Death in the Rational World of Defense Intellectuals." *Signs* 12, no. 4 (1987): 687–718.

Cole, Paul M. "Atomic Bombast: Nuclear Weapon Decision-Making in Sweden, 1945–1972." Stimson Center Occasional Paper 26, 1996.

Committee for the Compilation of Materials on Damage Caused by the Atomic Bombs in Hiroshima and Nagasaki. *Hiroshima and Nagasaki: The Physical, Medical, and Social Effects of the Atomic Bombings*. Translated by Eisei Ishikawa and David L. Swain. New York: Basic Books, 1981.

Committee on International Security and Arms Control, National Academy of Sciences. *The Future of U.S. Nuclear Weapons Policy*. Washington, DC: National Academy Press, 1997.

Copeland, Dale C. *The Origins of Major War.* Ithaca, NY: Cornell University Press, 2000.

Craig, Campbell. *Destroying the Village: Eisenhower and Thermonuclear War.* New York: Columbia University Press, 1998.

Craig, Gordon A., and Alexander L. George. *Force and Statecraft: Diplomatic Problems of Our Time.* New York: Oxford University Press, 1983.

Creveld, Martin van. *Technology and War: From 2000 B.C. to the Present.* New York: Free Press, 1991.

Culbertson, Ely. *Total Peace: What Makes Wars and How to Organize Peace.* Garden City, NY: Doubleday, Doran, 1943.

Cullings, Harry M., Shoichiro Fujita, Sachiyo Funamoto, Eric J. Grant, George D. Kerr, and Dale L. Preston. "Dose Estimation for Atomic Bomb Survivor Studies: Its Evolution and Present Status." *Radiation Research* 166 (2006): 219–54.

Dahl, Curtis. "The American School of Catastrophe." *American Quarterly* 11, no. 3 (1959): 380–90.

Daley, Tad. *Apocalypse Never: Forging the Path to a Nuclear Weapon–Free World.* New Brunswick, NJ: Rutgers University Press, 2010.

Daly, Nicholas. "The Volcanic Disaster Narrative: From Pleasure Garden to Canvas, Page, and Stage." *Victorian Studies* 53, no. 2 (2011): 255–85.

Damasio, Antonio. *Descartes' Error: Emotion, Reason, and the Human Brain.* London: Vintage Books, 2006.

Davison, W. Phillips. *The Berlin Blockade: A Study in Cold War Politics.* Princeton, NJ: Princeton University Press, 1958.

DeGroot, Gerard J. *The Bomb: A Life.* Cambridge, MA: Harvard University Press, 2005.

Deitchman, Seymour J. *On Being a Superpower and Not Knowing What to Do About It.* Boulder, CO: Westview Press, 2000.

DeNardo, James. *The Amateur Strategist: Intuitive Deterrence Theories and the Politics of the Nuclear Arms Race.* New York: Cambridge University Press, 1995.

Dingman, Roger. "Atomic Diplomacy During the Korean War." *International Security* 13, no. 3 (Winter 1988): 50–91.

Dobbs, Michael. *One Minute to Midnight: Kennedy, Khrushchev, and Castro on the Brink of Nuclear War.* New York: Vintage Books, 2009.

Dower, John W. *Cultures of War: Pearl Harbor, Hiroshima, 9-11, Iraq.* New York: W. W. Norton, 2010.

——. *Japan in War and Peace: Selected Essays.* New York: New Press, 1993.

——. *War Without Mercy: Race and Power in the Pacific War.* New York: Pantheon Books, 1986.

Draper, Theodore. *Present History: On Nuclear War, Detente, and Other Controversies.* New York: Random House, 1983.

Drea, Edward J. *In the Service of the Emperor: Essays on the Imperial Japanese Army.* Lincoln: University of Nebraska Press, 1998.

Dumas, Lloyd J. *Lethal Arrogance: Human Fallibility and Dangerous Technologies.* New York: St. Martin's Press, 1999.

Dyson, Freeman. *Disturbing the Universe.* New York: Harper Colophon Books, 1979.

———. *Weapons and Hope.* New York: Harper and Row, 1984.

Earle, Edward Mead, ed. *Maker of Modern Strategy: Military Thought from Machiavelli to Hitler.* Princeton, NJ: Princeton University Press, 1941.

Eden, Lynn. "City on Fire." *Bulletin of the Atomic Scientists* 60, no. 1 (2004): 33–43.

———. *Whole World on Fire: Organizations, Knowledge, and Nuclear Weapons Devastation.* Ithaca, NY: Cornell University Press, 2004.

Eden, Lynn, and Steven E. Miller, eds. *Nuclear Arguments: Understanding the Strategic Nuclear Arms and Arms Control Debates.* Ithaca, NY: Cornell University Press, 1989.

Edgerton, David. *The Shock of the Old: Technology and Global History Since 1900.* New York: Oxford University Press, 2007.

Ehrenreich, Barbara. *Blood Rites.* New York: Henry Holt, 1997.

ElBaradei, Mohamed. *The Age of Deception: Nuclear Diplomacy in Treacherous Times.* New York: Metropolitan Books, 2011.

Elshtain, Jean Bethke, ed. *Just War Theory.* New York: New York University Press, 1992.

Enthoven, Alain C., and K. Wayne Smith. *How Much Is Enough?: Shaping the Defense Program, 1961–1969.* Santa Monica, CA: RAND Corporation, 2005.

Etzold, Thomas H., and John Lewis Gaddis, eds. *Containment: Documents on American Policy and Strategy, 1945–1950.* New York: Columbia University Press, 1978.

Executive Office of the Statistics Commission and Statistics Bureau of the Prime Minister's Office. *Japan Statistical Yearbook 1949.* Nihon: Mainichi Shinbunsha, 1949.

Falk, Richard A., Gabriel Kolko, and Robert Jay Lifton, eds. *Crimes of War: A Legal Political-Documentary, and Psychological Inquiry into the Responsibility of Leaders, Citizens, and Soldiers for Criminal Acts in War.* New York: Vintage Books, 1971.

Feis, Herbert. *The Atomic Bomb and the End of World War II.* Rev. ed. Princeton, NJ: Princeton University Press, 1966.

Feiveson, Harold A., ed. *The Nuclear Turning Point: A Blueprint for Deep Cuts and De-Alerting of Nuclear Weapons.* Washington, DC: Brookings Institution Press, 1999.

Feldbaum, Carl B., and Ronald J. Bee. *Looking the Tiger in the Eye: Confronting the Nuclear Threat.* New York: Vintage Books, 1990.

Fields, Rick. *The Code of the Warrior in History, Myth, and Everyday Life.* New York: Harper Perennial, 1991.

Fierke, K. M. *Critical Approaches to International Security.* Malden, MA: Polity Press, 2007.

———. "Whereof We Can Speak, Thereof We Must Not Be Silent: Trauma, Political Solipsism and War." *Review of International Studies* 30, no. 4 (2004): 471–91.

Finkbeiner, Ann. *The Jasons: The Secret History of Science's Postwar Elite.* New York: Viking, 2006.

Fischer, John. *Why They Behave Like Russians.* New York: Harper and Brothers, 1947.

Foard, James H. "Imagining Nuclear Weapons: Hiroshima, Armageddon, and the Annihilation of the Students of Ichijo School." *Journal of the American Academy of Religion* 65, no. 1 (1997): 1–18.

Foot, Rosemary J. "Nuclear Coercion and the Ending of the Korean Conflict." *International Security* 13, no. 3 (Winter 1988/1989): 92–112.

Ford, Daniel. *The Cult of the Atom: The Secret Papers of the Atomic Energy Commission.* New York: Simon and Schuster, 1982.

Ford, Daniel, Henry Kendall, and Steven Nadis. *Beyond the Freeze: The Road to Nuclear Sanity.* Boston: Beacon Press, 1982.

Frank, Richard B. *Downfall: The End of the Imperial Japanese Empire.* New York: Random House, 1999.

Frankland, Mark. *Khrushchev.* New York: Stein and Day, 1979.

Freedman, Lawrence. *Britain and Nuclear Weapons.* London: Macmillan Press, 1980.

———. *The Evolution of Nuclear Strategy.* New York: St. Martin's Press, 1981.

———. *U.S. Intelligence and the Soviet Strategic Threat.* 2nd ed. Princeton, NJ: Princeton University Press, 1986.

Freedman, Lawrence, ed. *War.* New York: Oxford University Press, 1994.

Friedman, George, and Meredith Friedman. *The Future of War: Power, Technology, and American World Dominance in the Twenty-First Century.* New York: St. Martin's Press, 1996.

Friedman, Jeffrey, ed. *The Rational Choice Controversy: Economic Models of Politics Reconsidered.* New Haven, CT: Yale University Press, 1996.

Friedman, Leon, and William F. Levantrosser, eds. *Richard M. Nixon: Politician, President, Administrator.* New York: Greenwood Press, 1991.

Fussell, Paul. *The Great War and Modern Memory.* New York: Oxford University Press, 1975.

———. *Thank God for the Atom Bomb and Other Essays*. New York: Ballantine Books, 1988.

———. *Wartime: Understanding and Behavior in the Second World War*. New York: Oxford University Press, 1989.

Gaddis, John Lewis. *The Cold War: A New History*. New York: Penguin Press, 2005.

———. "The Long Peace: Elements of Stability in the Postwar International System." *International Security* 10, no. 4 (Spring 1986): 99–142.

———. *The Long Peace: Inquiries into the History of the Cold War*. Oxford: Oxford University Press, 1987.

———. *Strategies of Containment: A Critical Appraisal of Postwar American National Security Policy*. New York: Oxford University Press, 1982.

Gaddis, John Lewis, Philip H. Gordon, Ernest R. May, and Jonathan Rosenberg, eds. *Cold War Statesmen Confront the Bomb: Nuclear Diplomacy Since 1945*. Oxford: Oxford University Press, 1999.

Gardner, Dan. *Risk: The Science and Politics of Fear*. Toronto: McClelland and Stewart, 2008.

Gardner, John W., and Francesca Gardner Reese, eds. *Quotations of Wit and Wisdom: Know or Listen to Those Who Know*. New York: W. W. Norton, 1975.

Garthoff, Raymond L. "Cuban Missile Crisis: The Soviet Story." *Foreign Policy* 72 (1988): 61–80.

———. *Intelligence Assessment and Policymaking: A Decision Point in the Kennedy Administration*. Washington, DC: Brookings Institution, 1984.

———. *Perspectives on the Strategic Balance*. Washington, DC: Brookings Institution, 1983.

———. *Reflections on the Cuban Missile Crisis*. Rev. ed. Washington, DC: Brookings Institution, 1989.

Geller, Daniel S. "Nuclear Weapons, Deterrence, and Crisis Escalation." *Journal of Conflict Resolution* 34, no. 2 (1990): 291–310.

Gelvin, Michael. *War and Existence: A Philosophical Inquiry*. University Park: Pennsylvania State University Press, 1994.

George, Alexander L., and Richard Smoke. *Deterrence in American Foreign Policy: Theory and Practice*. New York: Columbia University Press, 1974.

Ginzburg, Carlo. *Clues, Myths, and the Historical Method*. Translated by John Tedeschi and Anne C. Tedeschi. Baltimore: Johns Hopkins University Press, 1992.

Giovannitti, Len, and Fred Freed. *The Decision to Drop the Bomb*. New York: Coward-McCann, 1965.

Glaser, Charles L. *Analyzing Strategic Nuclear Policy*. Princeton, NJ: Princeton University Press, 1990.

——. "Nuclear Policy Without an Adversary: U.S. Planning for the Post-Soviet Era." *International Security* 16, no. 4 (1992): 34–78.

Gordin, Michael D. *Red Cloud at Dawn: Truman, Stalin, and the End of the Atomic Monopoly.* New York: Farrar, Straus and Giroux, 2009.

Gormley, Dennis M. *Missile Contagion: Cruise Missile Proliferation and the Threat to International Security.* Westport, CT: Praeger Security International, 2008.

Gottfried, Kurt, and Bruce G. Blair, eds. *Crisis Stability and Nuclear War.* New York: Oxford University Press, 1988.

Gottschall, Jonathan. *The Storytelling Animal: How Stories Make Us Human.* Boston: Houghton Mifflin Harcourt, 2012.

Graham, Bob, Jim Talent, Allison Graham, Robin Cleveland, Steve Rademaker, Tim Roemer, Wendy Sherman, Henry Sokolski, and Rich Verma. *World at Risk: The Report of the Commission on the Prevention of Weapons of Mass Destruction Proliferation and Terrorism.* New York: Vintage Books, 2008.

Graham, Thomas, Jr., and Keith A. Hansen. *Spy Satellites and Other Intelligence Technologies That Changed History.* Seattle: University of Washington Press, 2007.

Grattan, John, and Robin Torrence, eds. *Living Under the Shadow: The Cultural Impacts of Volcano Eruptions.* Walnut Creek, CA: Left Coast Press, 2007.

Gray, Colin S., and Keith Payne. "Victory Is Possible." *Foreign Policy* 39 (1980): 14–27.

Gray, J. Glenn. *On Understanding Violence Philosophically and Other Essays.* New York: Harper and Row, 1970.

——. *The Warriors: Reflections on Men in Battle.* Lincoln: University of Nebraska Press, 1998.

Grayling, A. C. *Among the Dead Cities: The History and Moral Legacy of the WWII Bombing of Civilians in Germany and Japan.* New York: Walker, 2006.

Green, Robert. *Naked Nuclear Emperor: Debunking Nuclear Deterrence.* Christchurch, New Zealand: Disarmament and Security Centre, 2000.

——. *Security Without Nuclear Deterrence.* Christchurch, New Zealand: Astron Media and Disarmament and Security Centre, 2010.

Greene, Owen, Ian Percival, and Irene Ridge. *Nuclear Winter.* New York: Polity Press, 1985.

Gregory, Donna. *The Nuclear Predicament: A Sourcebook.* New York: St. Martin's Press, 1986.

Grinspoon, Lester, ed. *The Long Darkness: Psychological and Moral Perspectives on Nuclear Winter.* New Haven, CT: Yale University Press, 1986.

Grunden, Walter E., Mark Walker, and Masakatsu Yamazaki. "Wartime Nuclear Weapons Research in Germany and Japan." *Osiris* 20 (2005): 107–30.

Guillemin, Jeanne. *Biological Weapons: From the Invention of State-Sponsored Programs to Contemporary Bioterrorism*. New York: Columbia University Press, 2005.

Gusterson, Hugh. "Nuclear Weapons and the Other in the Western Imagination." *Cultural Anthropology* 14, no. 1 (1999): 111–43.

Hachiya, Michihiko. *Hiroshima Diary: The Journal of a Japanese Physician, August 6–September 30, 1945*. Translated and edited by Warner Wells. New York: University of North Carolina Press, 1955.

Hackett, John. *The Third World War: August 1985*. New York: Macmillan, 1978.

Haley, P. Edward, David M. Keithly, and Jack Merritt, eds. *Nuclear Strategy, Arms Control, and the Future*. Boulder, CO: Westview Press, 1985.

Hallett, Brien. *The Lost Art of Declaring War*. Chicago: University of Illinois Press, 1998.

Halperin, Morton H. *Nuclear Fallacy: Dispelling the Myth of Nuclear Strategy*. Cambridge: Ballinger, 1987.

Hanson, Victor Davis. *The Western Way of War: Infantry Battle in Classical Greece*. Berkeley: University of California Press, 1989.

Hare, J. E., and Carey B. Joynt. *Ethics and International Affairs*. New York: St. Martin's Press, 1982.

Harrington de Santana, Anne. "The Strategy of Non-Proliferation: Maintaining the Credibility of an Incredible Pledge to Disarm." *Millennium* 40, no. 3 (September 2011): 3–19.

———. *Strategy*. 2nd rev. ed. New York: Frederick A. Praeger, 1968.

Hasegawa, Tsuyoshi. *The End of the Pacific War: Reappraisals*. Stanford, CA: Stanford University Press, 2007.

———. *Racing the Enemy: Stalin, Truman, and the Surrender of Japan*. Cambridge, MA: Belknap Press of Harvard University Press, 2005.

Hastings, Max. *Armageddon: The Battle for Germany, 1944–1945*. New York: Vintage Books, 2005.

———. *The Oxford Book of Military Anecdotes*. New York: Oxford University Press, 2002.

———. *Retribution: The Battle for Japan, 1944–1945*. New York: Vintage Books, 2009.

Hedges, Chris. *War Is a Force That Gives Us Meaning*. New York: Anchor Books, 2003.

Henkin, Louis, ed. *Arms Control: Issues for the Public*. Englewood Cliffs, NJ: Spectrum, 1961.

——. *Foreign Affairs and the Constitution.* New York: W. W. Norton, 1975.

Herken, Gregg. *The Winning Weapon: The Atomic Bomb in the Cold War, 1945–1950.* New York: Vintage Books, 1982.

Hersey, John. *Hiroshima.* New York: Bantam Books, 1981.

Herzog, Chaim. *The Arab-Israeli Wars: War and Peace in the Middle East from the 1948 War of Independence to the Present.* New York: Vintage Books, 2004.

Hewitt, Kenneth. "Place Annihilation: Area Bombing and the Fate of Urban Places." *Annals of the Association of American Geographers* 73, no. 2 (1983): 257–84.

Hicks, David. Review. *Anthropos* 94 (1999): 593–94.

Hillman, James. *A Terrible Love of War.* New York: Penguin Books, 2005.

Hilsman, Roger. *To Move a Nation: The Politics of Foreign Policy in the Administration of John F. Kennedy.* Garden City, NY: Doubleday, 1967.

Hitchens, Theresa. "Space Wars." *Scientific American* 298 (March 2008): 78–85.

Hoffman, Bruce. *Inside Terrorism.* Rev. ed. New York: Columbia University Press, 2006.

Hoffman, David E. *The Dead Hand: The Untold Story of the Cold War Arms Race and Its Dangerous Legacy.* New York: Doubleday, 2009.

Hogan, Michael J., ed. *The Ambiguous Legacy: U.S. Foreign Relations in the "American Century."* New York: Cambridge University Press, 1999.

——. *Hiroshima in History and Memory.* New York: Cambridge University Press, 1997.

Holloway, David, *The Soviet Union and the Arms Race.* New Haven, CT: Yale University Press, 1983.

Homer. *The Iliad.* Translated by Robert Fagles. New York: Penguin Books, 1990.

Horelick, Arnold L., ed. *U.S.-Soviet Relations: The Next Phase.* Ithaca, NY: Cornell University Press, 1986.

Howard, Michael. *The Causes of Wars.* 2nd ed. Cambridge, MA: Harvard University Press, 1984.

——. *Clausewitz.* New York: Oxford University Press, 1983.

——. *War and the Liberal Conscience.* New York: Columbia University Press, 2008.

Howard, Robert Glenn. "Apocalypse in Your In-Box: End-Times Communication on the Internet." *Western Folklore* 56 (Summer/Fall 1997): 295–315.

Huntington, Samuel P. *The Common Defense: Strategic Programs in National Politics.* New York: Columbia University Press, 1966.

Hymans, Jacques E. C. *The Psychology of Nuclear Proliferation: Identity, Emotions, and Foreign Policy.* Cambridge: Cambridge University Press, 2006.

Ignatieff, Michael, and Amy Gutmann, eds. *Human Rights as Politics and Idolatry*. Princeton, NJ: Princeton University Press, 2001.

Iklé, Fred Charles. *The Social Impact of Bomb Destruction*. Norman: University of Oklahoma Press, 1958.

International Panel on Fissile Materials. *Reducing and Eliminating Nuclear Weapons: Country Perspectives on the Challenges to Nuclear Disarmament*. Princeton, NJ: Report for Princeton University, May 2010.

Isaacson, Walter, and Evan Thomas. *The Wise Men: Six Men and the World They Made*. New York: Touchstone, 1988.

James, William. *William James: Pragmatism and Other Writings*. New York: Penguin Books, 2000.

Janis, Irving L. *Air War and Emotional Stress: Psychological Studies of Bombing and Civilian Defense*. New York: McGraw-Hill, 1951.

Jarecki, Eugene. *The American Way of War: Guided Missiles, Misguided Men, and a Republic in Peril*. New York: Free Press, 2008.

Jensen, Lloyd. *Negotiating Nuclear Arms Control*. Columbia: University of South Carolina Press, 1988.

Jervis, Robert. "The Future of World Politics: Will It Resemble the Past?" *International Security* 16, no. 3 (1991): 39–73.

———. *The Illogic of American Nuclear Strategy*. Ithaca, NY: Cornell University Press, 1984.

———. "Political Psychology — Some Challenges and Opportunities." *Political Psychology* 10, no. 3 (1989): 481–93.

Jervis, Robert, Richard Ned Lebow, and Janice Gross Stein. *Psychology and Deterrence*. Baltimore: Johns Hopkins University Press, 1991.

Joffe, Josef, and James W. Davis. "Less Than Zero: Bursting the New Disarmament Bubble." *Foreign Affairs* 90, no. 1 (2011): 7–13.

Johnson, James Turner. *Just War Tradition and the Restraint of War: A Moral and Historical Inquiry*. Princeton, NJ: Princeton University Press, 1981.

Joseph, Robert G., and John F. Reichart. "The Case for Nuclear Deterrence Today." *Orbis* 42, no. 1 (1998): 7–13.

Jungk, Robert. *Brighter Than a Thousand Suns: A Personal History of the Atomic Scientists*. New York: Harcourt, Brace and World, 1958.

Kagan, Donald. *On the Origins of War and the Preservation of Peace*. New York: Anchor Books, 1995.

Kahn, Herman. *On Escalation: Metaphors and Scenarios*. New York: Frederick A. Praeger, 1965.

———. *On Thermonuclear War*. Princeton, NJ: Princeton University Press, 1960.

Kaku, Michio, and Daniel Axelrod. *To Win a Nuclear War: The Pentagon's Secret War Plans*. Boston: South End Press, 1987.

Kaplan, Fred. *The Wizards of Armageddon.* New York: Simon and Schuster, 1983.

Kaplan, Stephen S. *Diplomacy of Power: Soviet Armed Forces as a Political Instrument.* Washington, DC: Brookings Institution, 1981.

Karp, Regina Cowen, ed. *Security Without Nuclear Weapons?: Different Perspectives on Non-Nuclear Security.* New York: Oxford University Press, 1992.

Katz, Arthur M. *Life After Nuclear War: The Economic and Social Impacts of Nuclear Attacks on the United States.* Cambridge, MA: Ballinger, 1982.

Keefer, Edward C. "President Dwight D. Eisenhower and the End of the Korean War." *Diplomatic History* 10, no. 3 (July 1986): 267–89.

Keegan, John. *The Face of Battle: A Study of Agincourt, Waterloo, and the Somme.* New York: Vintage Books, 1977.

———. *A History of Warfare.* New York: Alfred A. Knopf, 1993.

Kegley, Charles W., Jr., and Eugene R. Wittkopf. *The Nuclear Reader: Strategy, Weapons, War.* 2nd ed. New York: St. Martin's Press, 1989.

Kennan, George F. *At a Century's Ending: Reflections, 1982–1995.* New York: W. W. Norton, 1996.

———. *The Fateful Alliance: France, Russia, and the Coming of the First World War.* New York: Pantheon Books, 1984.

———. *The Nuclear Delusion: Soviet-American Relations in the Atomic Age.* New York: Pantheon Books, 1983.

Kennedy, John F. *Public Papers of the Presidents of the United States: John F. Kennedy, 1963.* Washington, DC: Government Printing Office, 1964.

Kennedy, Paul, ed. *Grand Strategies in War and Peace.* New Haven, CT: Yale University Press, 1991.

Kennedy, Robert F. *Thirteen Days: A Memoir of the Cuban Missile Crisis.* New York: Signet Books, 1969.

———. *To Seek a Newer World.* New York: Bantam Books, 1967.

Keohane, Robert O., Stanley Hoffmann, and Joseph Nye, eds. *After the Cold War: International Institutions and State Strategies in Europe, 1989–1991.* Cambridge, MA: Harvard University Press, 1993.

Kerblay, Basile. *Modern Soviet Society.* Translated by Rupert Swyer. New York: Pantheon Books, 1983.

Kier, Elizabeth. *Imagining War: French and British Military Doctrine Between the Wars.* Princeton, NJ: Princeton University Press, 1997.

Kincade, William H. "Arms Control or Arms Coercion?" *Foreign Policy* 62 (Spring 1986): 24–45.

King-Hall, Stephen. *Defence in the Nuclear Age.* London: Camelot Press, 1958.

Kissinger, Henry A. *Ending the Vietnam War: A History of America's Involvement in and Extrication from the Vietnam War.* New York: Simon and Schuster, 2003.

———. "Reflections on Cuba." *Reporter,* November 22, 1962, 21–24.

———. *A World Restored: Metternich, Castlereagh, and the Problems of Peace.* Boston: Houghton Mifflin, 1957.

Kort, Michael, ed. *The Columbia Guide to Hiroshima and the Bomb.* New York: Columbia University Press, 2007.

Krajick, Kevin. "Tracking Myth to Geological Reality." *Science* 310 (2005): 762–64.

Kramer, Mark. "Correspondence: Remembering the Cuban Missile Crisis: Should We Swallow Oral History?" *International Security* 15, no. 1 (1990): 212–18.

Kugler, Jacek. "Terror Without Deterrence: Reassessing the Role of Nuclear Weapons." *Journal of Conflict Resolution* 28, no. 3 (1984): 470–506.

Kull, Steven. *Minds at War: Nuclear Reality and the Inner Conflicts of Defense Policymakers.* New York: Basic Books, 1982.

———. "Nuclear Arms and the Desire for World Destruction." *Political Psychology* 4, no. 3 (1983): 563–91.

Kull, Steven, Clay Ramsay, Stefan Subias, and Evan Lewis. *Americans on WMD Proliferation.* Program on International Policy Attitudes (PIPA) and Knowledge Networks, 2004.

Lake, Anthony. *The Vietnam Legacy: The War, American Society, and the Future of American Foreign Policy.* New York: New York University Press, 1976.

Lambek, Michael, ed. *A Reader in the Anthropology of Religion.* 2nd ed. Malden, MA: Blackwell, 2008.

Lamont, Lansing. *Day of Trinity.* New York: Atheneum, 1985.

Lange, David. *Nuclear Free—the New Zealand Way.* New York: Penguin Books, 1990.

Lapp, Ralph. *Atoms and People.* New York: Harper and Brothers, 1956.

———. *Kill and Overkill: The Strategy of Annihilation.* New York: Basic Books, 1962.

Larkin, Bruce D. *Designing Denuclearization: An Interpretive Encyclopedia.* New Brunswick, NJ: Transaction, 2008.

Lavoy, Peter R. "Predicting Nuclear Proliferation: A Declassified Documentary Record." *Strategic Insights* 3, no. 1 (January 2004).

Lawry, Walter. *We Said No to War!* Dunedin, New Zealand: Wordspinners Unlimited, 1994.

Lebow, Richard Ned. *Between Peace and War: The Nature of International Crisis.* Baltimore: Johns Hopkins University Press, 1984.

———. "The Cuban Missile Crisis: Reading the Lessons Correctly." *Political Science Quarterly* 98, no. 3 (Fall 1983): 431–58.

Lebow, Richard Ned, and Janice Gross Stein. *We All Lost the Cold War.* Princeton, NJ: Princeton University Press, 1994.

Lederberg, Joshua, ed. *Biological Weapons: Limiting the Threat.* Cambridge, MA: MIT Press, 2001.

Lee, Steven P. *Morality, Prudence, and Nuclear Weapons.* New York: Cambridge University Press, 1996.

Lefever, Ernest W., and E. Stephen Hunt. "Education, Propaganda, and Nuclear Arms." *Phi Delta Kappan* 64, no. 10 (1983): 727–28.

Lefever, Ernest W., and E. Stephen Hunt, eds. *The Apocalyptic Premise: Nuclear Arms Debated.* Washington, DC: Ethics and Public Policy Center, 1982.

Lehrer, Jonah. *How We Decide.* Boston: Mariner Books, 2010.

LeMay, Curtis E., and MacKinlay Kantor. *Mission with LeMay: My Story.* Garden City, NY: Doubleday, 1965.

Lerner, Max. *The Age of Overkill: A Preface to World Politics.* New York: Simon and Schuster, 1962.

Levene, Mark, and Penny Roberts, eds. *The Massacre in History.* New York: Berghahn Books, 1999.

Levi, Michael. *On Nuclear Terrorism.* Cambridge, MA: Harvard University Press, 2007.

Levine, Alan J. *The Strategic Bombing of Germany, 1940–1945.* Westport, CT: Praeger, 1992.

Lévy, Bernard-Henri. *War, Evil, and the End of History.* Translated by Charlotte Mandell. Hoboken, NJ: Melville House, 2004.

Levy, Jack S., and William R. Thompson. *Causes of War.* Malden, MA: Wiley-Blackwell, 2010.

Lewis, Jeffrey. *The Minimum Means of Reprisal: China's Search for Security in the Nuclear Age.* Cambridge, MA: American Academy of Arts and Sciences, 2007.

Lewis, Patricia, Ken Berry, Benoît Pelopidas, Nikolai Sokov, and Ward Wilson, *Delegitimizing Nuclear Weapons: Examining the Validity of Nuclear Deterrence.* Monterey, CA: Center for Nonproliferation Studies, 2010.

Liddell Hart, B. H. *History of the Second World War.* New York: Capricorn Books, 1972.

Lifton, Robert Jay. *The Future of Immortality and Other Essays for a Nuclear Age.* New York: Basic Books, 1987.

——. "Illusions of the Second Nuclear Age." *World Policy Journal* 18, no. 1 (2001): 25–30.

——. "In the Lord's Hands: America's Apocalyptic Mindset." *World Policy Journal* 20, no. 3 (2003): 59–69.

Lifton, Robert Jay, and Eric Markusen. *The Genocidal Mentality: Nazi Holocaust and Nuclear Threat.* New York: Basic Books, 1990.

Lilienthal, David E. *Change, Hope, and the Bomb.* Princeton, NJ: Princeton University Press, 1963.

Lincoln, Abraham. *Speeches and Writings, 1832–1858: Speeches, Letters, and Miscellaneous Writings.* New York: Library of America, 1989.

Lindqvist, Sven. *A History of Bombing.* Translated by Linda Haverty Rugg. New York: New Press, 2001.

Linenthal, Edward T., and Tom Engelhardt. *History Wars: The Enola Gay and Other Battles for the American Past.* New York: Metropolitan Books, 1996.

Livingston, Jon, Joe Moore, and Felicia Oldfather, eds. *Imperial Japan, 1800–1945.* New York: Pantheon Books, 1973.

Luard, Evan. *The Blunted Sword: The Erosion of Military Power in Modern World Politics.* New York: New Amsterdam Books, 1988.

Luttwak, Edward N. *On the Meaning of Victory: Essays on Strategy.* New York: Simon and Schuster, 1986.

Lynn-Jones, Sean M., and Steven Miller, eds. *The Cold War and After: Prospects for Peace.* Rev. ed. Cambridge, MA: MIT Press, 1994.

Machiavelli, Niccolò. *The Art of War.* Translated by Ellis Farneworth. New York: Da Capo Press, 1965.

MacIsaac, David. *Strategic Bombing in World War Two: The Story of the United States Strategic Bombing Survey.* New York: Garland, 1976.

Mack, John E. "Nuclear Weapons and the Dark Side of Humankind." *Political Psychology* 7, no. 2 (1986): 223–33.

———. "Toward a Collective Psychopathology of the Nuclear Arms Competition." *Political Psychology* 6, no. 2 (1985): 291–321.

Maddox, Robert James, ed. *Hiroshima in History: The Myths of Revisionism.* Columbia: University of Missouri Press, 2007.

———. *Weapons for Victory: The Hiroshima Decision Fifty Years Later.* Columbia: University of Missouri Press, 1995.

Malcolmson, Robert W. *Nuclear Fallacies: How We Have Been Misguided Since Hiroshima.* Montreal: McGill Queen's University Press, 1985.

Malik, John S. *The Yields of Hiroshima and Nagasaki Nuclear Explosions.* Los Alamos, NM: Los Alamos National Laboratory, 1983.

Mandelbaum, Michael. *The Nuclear Question: The United States and Nuclear Weapons, 1946–1976.* New York: Cambridge University Press, 1979.

———. *The Nuclear Revolution: International Politics Before and After Hiroshima.* New York: Cambridge University Press, 1981.

Martin, Brian. "Critique of Nuclear Extinction." *Journal of Peace Research* 19, no. 4 (1982): 287–300.

May, Ernest R. "The United States, the Soviet Union, and the Far Eastern War, 1941–1945." *Pacific Historical Review* 24, no. 2 (May 1955): 153–74.

May, Ernest R., and Philip D. Zelikow, eds. *The Kennedy Tapes: Inside the White House During the Cuban Missile Crisis.* New York: W. W. Norton, 2002.

May, Larry, ed. *War: Essays in Political Philosophy.* New York: Cambridge University Press, 2008.

Mayor, Adrienne. *Greek Fire, Poison Arrows, and Scorpion Bombs: Biological and Chemical Warfare in the Ancient World.* New York: Overlook Press, 2004.

Mazarr, Michael J., ed. *Nuclear Weapons in a Transformed World.* New York: St. Martin's Press, 1997.

McConeghey, Evelyn, and James McConnell, eds. *Nuclear Reactions.* Albuquerque: Image Seminars, 1984.

McMahon, Robert J. *The Cold War.* New York: Oxford University Press, 2003.

McNamara, Robert S. *Blundering into Disaster: Surviving the First Century of the Nuclear Age.* New York: Pantheon Books, 1987.

McNamara, Robert S., and James G. Blight. *Wilson's Ghost: Reducing the Risk of Conflict, Killing, and Catastrophe in the Twenty-First Century.* New York: Public Affairs, 2003.

McNeill, William H. *The Pursuit of Power.* Chicago: University of Chicago Press, 1982.

Melman, Seymour. *The Permanent War Economy: American Capitalism in Decline.* New York: Touchstone Books, 1974.

Mendlovitz, Saul H., and Barbara Walker, eds. *A Reader on Second Assembly and Parliamentary Proposals.* Wayne, NJ: Center for UN Reform Education, 2003.

Merli, Frank J., and Theodore Wilson, eds. *Makers of American Diplomacy: From Theodore Roosevelt to Henry Kissinger.* New York: Charles Scribner's Sons, 1974.

Michie, Allan A. *The Air Offensive Against Germany.* New York: Henry Holt, 1943.

Middleton, Drew. *Can America Win the Next War?* New York: Charles Scribner's Sons, 1975.

Miles, Rufus E., Jr. "Hiroshima: The Strange Myth of Half a Million American Lives Saved." *International Security* 10, no. 2 (1985): 121–40.

Miller, D. H. *The Geneva Protocol.* Oxford: Benediction Classics, 2011.

Miller, Jerry. *Stockpile: The Story Behind 10,000 Strategic Nuclear Weapons.* Annapolis, MD: Naval Institute Press, 2010.

Miller, Robert D. *Descent from Niitaka, 1941–1945: First Flag over Japan.* Jersey Shore, PA: Bullbrier Press, 2002.

Miller, Steven, ed. *Conventional Forces and American Defense Policy: An International Security Reader.* Princeton, NJ: Princeton University Press, 1986.

———. *The Star Wars Controversy: An International Security Reader.* Princeton, NJ: Princeton University Press, 1986.

———. *Strategy and Nuclear Deterrence: An International Security Reader.* Princeton, NJ: Princeton University Press, 1984.

Miscamble, Wilson D. *From Roosevelt to Truman: Potsdam, Hiroshima, and the Cold War.* New York: Cambridge University Press, 2007.

———. "Harry S. Truman, the Berlin Blockade, and the 1948 Election." *Presidential Studies Quarterly* 10, no. 3 (1980): 306–16.

Mitchell, William. *Winged Defense: The Development and Possibilities of Modern Air Power — Economic and Military.* New York: Dover, 1988.

Moore, Mike. *Twilight War: The Folly of U.S. Space Dominance.* Oakland, CA: Independent Institute, 2008.

Morgan, Forrest E. *Compellence and the Strategic Culture of Imperial Japan: Implications for Coercive Diplomacy in the Twenty-First Century.* London: Praeger, 2003.

Morgan, Patrick M. "New Directions in Deterrence Theory." In Avner Cohen and Steven Lee, eds., *Nuclear Weapons and the Future of Humanity: The Fundamental Questions.* Totowa, NJ: Rowman and Littlefield, 1986.

Mueller, John. *Atomic Obsession: Nuclear Alarmism from Hiroshima to Al-Qaeda.* New York: Oxford University Press, 2010.

———. *Retreat from Doomsday: The Obsolescence of Major War.* New York: Basic Books, 1989.

———. "War Has Almost Ceased to Exist: An Assessment." *Political Science Quarterly* 124, no. 2 (2009): 297–321.

Murray, Williamson, MacGregor Knox, and Alvin Bernstein, eds. *The Making of Strategy: Rulers, States, and War.* New York: Cambridge University Press, 2009.

Myrdal, Alva. *The Game of Disarmament: How the United States and Russia Run the Arms Race.* New York: Pantheon Books, 1976.

Nathan, James, ed. *The Cuban Missile Crisis Revisited.* New York: St. Martin's Press, 1992.

National Conference of Catholic Bishops. *The Challenge of Peace: God's Promise and Our Response.* Washington, DC: United States Catholic Conference, 1983.

Neillands, Robin. *The Bomber War: The Allied Air Offensive Against Nazi Germany.* New York: Overlook Press, 2001.

Newhouse, John. *War and Peace in the Nuclear Age.* New York: Alfred A. Knopf, 1989.

Newman, Robert P. *Enola Gay and the Court of History.* New York: P. Lang, 2004.

Nicholson, Michael. *Rationality and the Analysis of International Conflict.* New York: Cambridge University Press, 1992.

Nicolson, Harold. *The Evolution of Diplomacy.* New York: Collier Books, 1966.

Nielsen, Axel E., and William H. Walker, eds. *Warfare in Cultural Context: Practice, Agency, and the Archaeology of Violence.* Tucson: University of Arizona Press, 2009.

Nolan, Janne E. *An Elusive Consensus: Nuclear Weapons and American Security After the Cold War.* Washington, DC: Brookings Institution, 1999.

Norris, Robert S., and Hans M. Kristensen. "Global Nuclear Weapons Inventories, 1945–2010." *Bulletin of the Atomic Scientists* 66, no. 4 (2010): 77–83.

Novak, Michael. *Moral Clarity in the Nuclear Age.* Nashville: Thomas Nelson, 1983.

Nye, Joseph S., Jr. *Nuclear Ethics.* New York: Free Press, 1986.

Oates, Stephen B. *Abraham Lincoln: The Man Behind the Myths.* New York: Harper and Row, 1984.

———. *With Malice Toward None: The Life of Abraham Lincoln.* New York: Harper and Row, 1977.

O'Connell, Robert L. *Of Arms and Men: A History of War, Weapons, and Aggression.* New York: Oxford University Press, 1989.

———. *Ride of the Second Horseman: The Birth and Death of War.* New York: Oxford University Press, 1995.

Office of Technology Assessment, U.S. Congress. *The Effects of Nuclear War.* Washington, DC: U.S. Government Printing Office, 1979.

Ogilvie-White, Tanya, ed. *On Nuclear Deterrence: The Correspondence of Sir Michael Quinlan.* New York: Routledge, 2011.

O'Hanlon, Michael E. *A Skeptic's Case for Nuclear Disarmament.* Washington, DC: Brookings Institution, 2010.

Oldenbourg, Zoé. *Massacre at Montségur: A History of the Albigensian Crusade.* London: Phoenix Press, 2000.

Olson, Mancur. *The Logic of Collective Action: Public Goods and the Theory of Groups.* Cambridge, MA: Harvard University Press, 1971.

O'Neill, Bard E. *Insurgency and Terrorism: Inside Modern Revolutionary Warfare.* Dulles, VA: Brassey's, 1990.

Orend, Brian. *The Morality of War.* Orchard Park, NY: Broadview Press, 2006.

Orme, John. "Deterrence Failures: A Second Look." *International Security* 11, no. 4 (1987): 96–124.

Osada, Arata, ed. *Children of Hiroshima.* New York: Harper Colophon Books, 1982.

Palmer-Fernandez, Gabriel. *Deterrence and the Crisis in Moral Theory: An*

Analysis of the Moral Literature on the Nuclear Arms Debate. New York: Peter Lang, 1996.

Pape, Robert A. *Bombing to Win: Air Power and Coercion in War.* Ithaca, NY: Cornell University Press, 1996.

——. "Coercive Air Power in the Vietnam War." *International Security* 15, no. 2 (1990): 103–46.

——. "Why Japan Surrendered." *International Security* 18, no. 2 (Fall 1993): 154–201.

Paret, Peter. *Understanding War: Essays on Clausewitz and the History of Military Power.* Princeton, NJ: Princeton University Press, 1992.

Parkinson, Stuart. "Does Anybody Remember the Nuclear Winter?" *Scientists for Global Responsibility Newsletter* 27 (July 2003).

Paterson, Thomas G., ed. *The Origins of the Cold War.* Lexington, MA: D. C. Heath, 1974.

Paul, T. V., Richard J. Harknett, and James J. Wirtz, eds. *The Absolute Weapon Revisited: Nuclear Arms and the Emerging International Order.* Ann Arbor: University of Michigan Press, 2000.

Payne, Keith B. *Deterrence in the Second Nuclear Age.* Lexington: University Press of Kentucky, 1996.

Pearson, Simon. *A Brief History of the End of the World: Apocalyptic Beliefs from Revelation to Eco-Disaster.* London: Robinson, 2006.

Pellegrino, Charles. *The Last Train from Hiroshima: Survivors Look Back.* New York: Henry Holt, 2010.

Pelopidas, Benoît. "The Oracles of Proliferation: How Experts Maintain a Biased Historical Reading That Limits Policy Innovation." *Nonproliferation Review* 18, no. 1 (March 2011).

Perkovich, George, and James Acton, eds. *Abolishing Nuclear Weapons: A Debate.* Washington, DC: Carnegie Endowment for International Peace, 2009.

Perkovich, George, Jessica T. Mathews, Joseph Cirincione, Rose Gottemoeller, and Jon B. Wolfsthal. *Universal Compliance: A Strategy for Nuclear Security.* Washington, DC: Carnegie Endowment for International Peace, 2005.

Peterson, Jeannie. *The Aftermath: The Human and Ecological Consequences of Nuclear War.* New York: Pantheon Books, 1983.

Pifer, Steven, Richard C. Bush, Vanda Felbab-Brown, Martin S. Indyk, Michael E. O'Hanlon, and Kenneth M. Pollack. *U.S. Nuclear and Extended Deterrence: Considerations and Challenges.* Washington, DC: Brookings Institution, 2010.

Pinker, Steven. *The Better Angels of Our Nature: Why Violence Has Declined.* New York: Viking, 2012.

Popkin, Richard H. "The Triumphant Apocalypse and the Catastrophic Apocalypse." In Avner Cohen and Steven Lee, eds., *Nuclear Weapons and the Future of Humanity: The Fundamental Questions.* Totowa, NJ: Rowman and Littlefield, 1986.

Potter, Ralph B. *War and Moral Discourse.* Richmond: John Knox Press, 1973.

Powers, Thomas, and Ruthven Tremain. *Total War: What It Is, How It Got That Way.* New York: William Morrow, 1988.

Prados, John. *The Soviet Estimate: U.S. Intelligence Analysis and Soviet Strategic Forces.* Princeton, NJ: Princeton University Press, 1986.

Prins, Gwyn, ed. *The Nuclear Crisis Reader.* New York: Vintage Books, 1984.

Pusey, Merlo J. *The Way We Go to War.* Boston: Houghton Mifflin, 1969.

Quinlan, Michael. "The Future of Nuclear Weapons: Policy for Western Possessors." *International Affairs* 69, no. 3 (1993): 485–96.

———. *Thinking About Nuclear Weapons: Principles, Problems, Prospects.* Oxford: Oxford University Press, 2009.

Rabb, Theodore K. *The Thirty Years' War.* 2nd ed. Lanham, MD: University Press of America, 1981.

Rabe, Stephen G. "The Cuban Missile Crisis Revisited." *Irish Studies in International Affairs* 3, no. 3 (1991): 59–66.

Rakove, Milton L. *Arms and Foreign Policy in the Nuclear Age.* New York: Oxford University Press, 1972.

Raman, J. Sri. *Flashpoint: How the U.S., India, and Pakistan Brought the World to the Brink of Nuclear War.* Monroe, ME: Common Courage Press, 2004.

Ramana, M. V. "The Bomb of the Blue God." *South Asian Magazine for Action and Reflection* 13 (2001).

Rasler, Karen A., and William R. Thompson. *The Great Powers and Global Struggle, 1490–1990.* Lexington: University Press of Kentucky, 1994.

Regan, Geoffrey. *Military Anecdotes.* London: Carlton Books, 2002.

Renshon, Jonathan. "Assessing Capabilities in International Politics: Biased Overestimation and the Case of the Imaginary 'Missile Gap.'" *Journal of Strategic Studies* 32, no. 1 (2009): 115–47.

Rhodes, Richard. *The Making of the Atomic Bomb.* New York: Simon and Schuster, 1986.

———. "Nuclear Options." *New York Times,* May 15, 2005.

———. *The Twilight of the Bombs: Recent Challenges, New Dangers, and the Prospects for a World Without Nuclear Weapons.* New York: Alfred A. Knopf, 2010.

Ritchie, Nick, and Paul Ingram. "A Progressive Nuclear Policy." *RUSI Journal* 155, no. 2 (2010): 40–45.

Rosenthal, Peggy. "The Nuclear Mushroom Cloud as Cultural Image." *American Literary History* 3, no. 1 (1991): 63–92.

Ross, Ralph G., and Louis I. Bredvold, eds. *The Philosophy of Edmund Burke: A Selection of His Speeches and Writings*. Ann Arbor: University of Michigan Press, 1970.

Rothgeb, John M., Jr. *Defining Power: Influence and Force in the Contemporary International System*. New York: St. Martin's Press, 1993.

Rublee, Maria Rost. *Nonproliferation Norms: Why States Choose Nuclear Restraint*. Athens: University of Georgia Press, 2009.

Rusk, Dean, Robert McNamara, George W. Ball, Roswell L. Gilpatric, Theodore Sorensen, and McGeorge Bundy. "Essay: The Lessons of the Cuban Missile Crisis." *Time*, September 27, 1982, available at http://www.time.com/time/magazine/article/0,9171,925769-1,00.html.

Russet, Bruce M., ed. *Peace, War, and Numbers*. Beverly Hills: Sage Publications, 1972.

Sagan, Carl, and Richard Turco. *A Path Where No Man Thought: Nuclear Winter and the End of the Arms Race*. New York: Random House, 1990.

Sagan, Scott D. "Lessons of the Yom Kippur Alert." *Foreign Policy* 36 (1979): 160–77.

———. "Nuclear Alerts and Crisis Management." *International Security* 9, no. 4 (1985): 99–139.

———. "Why Do States Build Nuclear Weapons?: Three Models in Search of a Bomb." *International Security* 21, no. 3 (1996): 54–86.

Sagan, Scott D., and Jeremi Suri. "The Madman Nuclear Alert: Secrecy, Signaling, and Safety in October 1969." *International Security* 27, no. 4 (2003): 150–83.

Sagan, Scott D., and Kenneth N. Waltz. *The Spread of Nuclear Weapons: A Debate Renewed*. New York: W. W. Norton, 2003.

Sanger, David E. "Nuclear Reality: America Loses Bite." *New York Times*, February 20, 2005.

Sauer, Tom. "A Second Nuclear Revolution: From Nuclear Primacy to Post-Existential Deterrence." *Journal of Strategic Studies* 32, no. 5 (2009): 745–67.

Sayle, Murray. "Did the Bomb End the War?" *New Yorker*, July 31, 1995.

Schaffer, Ronald. "American Military Ethics in World War II: The Bombing of German Civilians." *Journal of American History* 67, no. 2 (1980): 318–34.

Scheer, Robert. *With Enough Shovels: Reagan, Bush, and Nuclear War*. New York: Random House, 1982.

Schell, Jonathan. *The Abolition*. New York: Alfred A. Knopf, 1984.

———. *The Fate of the Earth*. New York: Alfred A. Knopf, 1982.

———. *The Seventh Decade: The New Shape of Nuclear Danger*. New York: Metropolitan Books, 2007.

——. *The Unconquerable World: Power, Nonviolence, and the Will of the People*. New York: Metropolitan Books, 2003.

——. *The Unfinished Twentieth Century*. New York: Verso, 2001.

Schelling, Thomas C. *Arms and Influence*. New Haven, CT: Yale University Press, 1966.

——. *The Strategy of Conflict*. Cambridge, MA: Harvard University Press, 1980.

——. "A World Without Nuclear Weapons?" *Daedalus* 138, no. 4 (Fall 2009): 124–29.

Schlesinger, Arthur M., Jr. *A Thousand Days: John F. Kennedy in the White House*. Greenwich, CT: Fawcett Premier Books, 1965.

Schrecker, Ellen, ed. *Cold War Triumphalism: The Misuse of History After the Fall of Communism*. New York: New Press, 2004.

Schroeer, Dietrich. *Science, Technology, and the Nuclear Arms Race*. New York: John Wiley and Sons, 1984.

Schwartz, David N. *NATO's Nuclear Dilemmas*. Washington, DC: Brookings Institution, 1983.

Schwartz, Stephen I., ed. *Atomic Audit: The Costs and Consequences of U.S. Nuclear Weapons Since 1940*. Washington, DC: Brookings Institution, 1998.

Schwartz, Stephen I., and Deepti Choubey. *Nuclear Security Spending: Assessing Costs, Examining Priorities*. Washington, DC: Carnegie Endowment for International Peace, 2009.

Scoblic, J. Peter. *U.S. vs. Them: How a Half Century of Conservatism Has Undermined America's Security*. New York: Viking, 2008.

Scott, Len. *The Cuban Missile Crisis and the Threat of Nuclear War*. London: Continuum, 2007.

Scott, Len, and Steve Smith. "Lessons of October: Historians, Political Scientists, Policy-Makers, and the Cuban Missile Crisis." *International Affairs* 70, no. 4 (1994): 659–84.

Scoville, Herbert, Jr. *MX: Prescription for Disaster*. Cambridge, MA: MIT Press, 1982.

Seaborg, Glenn T. *Kennedy, Khrushchev, and the Test Ban*. Berkeley: University of California Press, 1981.

Seabury, Paul, and Angelo Codevilla. *War: Ends and Means*. New York: Basic Books, 1989.

Sebald, W. G. *On the Natural History of Destruction*. New York: Modern Library, 2004.

Sekimori, Gaynor, trans. *Hibakusha: Survivors of Hiroshima and Nagasaki*. Tokyo: Kosei, 1987.

Sen, Amartya. *Identity and Violence: The Illusion of Destiny*. New York: W. W. Norton, 2006.

Sethi, Manpreet, ed. *Towards a Nuclear Weapon Free World.* New Delhi: KW Publishers, 2009.

Seward, Desmond. *The Monks of War: The Military Religious Orders.* New York: Penguin Books, 1995.

Shapiro, Jerome F. *Atomic Bomb Cinema: The Apocalyptic Imagination on Film.* New York: Routledge, 2002.

Shepley, James. "How Dulles Averted War: Three Times, New Disclosures Show, He Brought U.S. Back from the Brink." *Life,* January 16, 1956.

Sherry, Michael S. *The Rise of American Air Power: The Creation of Armageddon.* New Haven, CT: Yale University Press, 1987.

Sherwin, Martin J. *A World Destroyed: The Atomic Bomb and the Grand Alliance.* New York: Vintage Books, 1977.

Shigemitsu, Mamoru. *Japan and Her Destiny.* New York: E. P. Dutton, 1958.

Shils, Edward A., and Morris Janowitz. "Cohesion and Disintegration in the Wehrmacht in World War II." *Public Opinion Quarterly* 12, no. 2 (1948): 280–315.

Shue, Henry, ed. *Nuclear Deterrence and Moral Restraint.* New York: Cambridge University Press, 1989.

Shultz, George P., William J. Perry, Henry A. Kissinger, and Sam Nunn. "A World Free of Nuclear Weapons." *Wall Street Journal,* January 4, 2007.

Sigal, Leon V. *Fighting to a Finish: The Politics of War Termination in the United States and Japan, 1945.* Ithaca, NY: Cornell University Press, 1988.

Simons, Anna. "War: Back to the Future." *Annual Review of Anthropology* 28 (1999): 73–108.

Siracusa, Joseph M. *Nuclear Weapons.* New York: Oxford University Press, 2008.

Skates, John Ray. *The Invasion of Japan: Alternative to the Bomb.* Columbia: University of South Carolina Press, 2000.

Smith, Dale O. "The Role of Airpower Since World War II." *Military Affairs* 19, no. 2 (1955): 71–76.

Smith, Derek D. *Deterring America: Rogue States and the Proliferation of Weapons of Mass Destruction.* New York: Cambridge University Press, 2006.

Smith, Rupert. *The Utility of Force: The Art of War in the Modern World.* New York: Alfred A. Knopf, 2007.

Smoke, Richard. *National Security and the Nuclear Dilemma: An Introduction to the American Experience.* Reading, MA: Addison-Wesley, 1984.

———. *War: Controlling Escalation.* Cambridge, MA: Harvard University Press, 1977.

Solingen, Etel. *Nuclear Logics: Contrasting Paths in East Asia and the Middle East.* Princeton, NJ: Princeton University Press, 2007.

Sorensen, Theodore C. *Kennedy.* New York: Bantam Books, 1966.

———. "Memorandum for the President," October 17, 1962. Sorensen Papers, John F. Kennedy Library, Boston, MA, box 48, Cuba folder.

Spiers, Edward M. *Chemical Warfare.* Chicago: University of Illinois Press, 1986.

Stavropoulos, Steven. *The Beginning of All Wisdom: Timeless Advice from the Ancient Greeks.* New York: Marlowe, 2003.

Steele, Jonathan. *Soviet Power: The Kremlin's Foreign Policy—Brezhnev to Chernenko.* New York: Simon and Schuster, 1984.

Steinbruner, John D., and Leon V. Sigal, eds. *Alliance Security: NATO and the No-First-Use Question.* Washington, DC: Brookings Institution, 1983.

Sterba, James P. *The Ethics of War and Nuclear Deterrence.* Belmont, CA: Wadsworth, 1985.

Stimson, Henry L. "The Decision to Use the Atomic Bomb." *Harper's Magazine* 194 (February 1947): 97–107.

Strozier, Charles B. *Apocalypse: On the Psychology of Fundamentalism in America.* Boston: Beacon Press, 1994.

Strozier, Charles B., and Laura Simich. "Christian Fundamentalism and Nuclear Threat." *Political Psychology* 12, no. 1 (1991): 81–96.

Subcommittee on Investigations and Oversight of the Committee on Science and Technology. *The Consequences of Nuclear War on the Global Environment.* Washington, DC: U.S. Government Printing Office, 1983.

Summers, Harry G., Jr. "Lessons: A Soldier's View." *Wilson Quarterly* 7, no. 3 (1983): 125–35.

Sun-Tzu. *The Art of War.* Translated by John Minford. New York: Penguin Books, 2002.

Szumski, Bonnie. *Nuclear War: Opposing Viewpoints.* St. Paul: Greenhaven Press, 1985.

Takaki, Ronald. *Hiroshima: Why America Dropped the Atomic Bomb.* Boston: Little, Brown, 1995.

Talbott, Strobe. *Deadly Gambits: The Reagan Administration and the Stalemate in Nuclear Arms Control.* New York: Alfred A. Knopf, 1984.

———. *The Russians and Reagan.* New York: Vintage Books, 1984.

Tanaka, Yuki, and Marilyn Young, eds. *Bombing Civilians: A Twentieth-Century History.* New York: New Press, 2009.

Tannenwald, Nina. *The Nuclear Taboo: The United States and the Non-Use of Nuclear Weapons Since 1945.* New York: Cambridge University Press, 2007.

Taylor, A.J.P. *A History of the First World War.* New York: Berkley Medallion Books, 1963.

Teller, Edward, and Allen Brown. *The Legacy of Hiroshima.* Garden City, NY: Doubleday, 1962.

Temes, Peter S. *The Just War: An American Reflection on the Morality of War in Our Time.* Chicago: Ivan R. Dee, 2003.

Tertrais, Bruno. "In Defense of Deterrence: The Relevance, Morality and Cost-Effectiveness of Nuclear Weapons." *Proliferation Papers* 39 (Fall 2011).

Thompson, E. P. *The Heavy Danger: Writings on War, Past and Future.* New York: Pantheon Books, 1985.

Thompson, E. P., and Dan Smith. *Protest and Survive.* New York: Monthly Review Press, 1981.

Togo, Shigenori. *The Cause of Japan.* Translated by Fumihiko Togo and Ben Bruce Blakeney. New York: Simon and Schuster, 1956.

Townshend, Charles. *The Oxford History of Modern War.* New York: Oxford University Press, 2000.

Trachtenberg, Marc. *A Constructed Peace: The Making of the European Settlement, 1945–1963.* Princeton, NJ: Princeton University Press, 1999.

———. *History and Strategy.* Princeton, NJ: Princeton University Press, 1991.

———. "The Influence of Nuclear Weapons in the Cuban Missile Crisis." *International Security* 10, no. 1 (Summer 1985): 137–203.

———. "A 'Wasting Asset': American Strategy and the Shifting Nuclear Balance, 1949–1954." *International Security* 13, no. 3 (1988): 5–49.

Tsipis, Kosta. *Arsenal: Understanding Weapons in the Nuclear Age.* New York: Simon and Schuster, 1983.

Tuchman, Barbara W. *The March of Folly: From Troy to Vietnam.* New York: Ballantine Books, 1984.

Tucker, Jonathan B. *War of Nerves: Chemical Warfare from World War I to Al-Qaeda.* New York: Pantheon Books, 2006.

Turnbull, Stephen. *Mongol Warrior, 1200–1350.* New York: Osprey, 2003.

Turner, Stansfield. *Caging the Nuclear Genie: An American Challenge for Global Security.* Boulder, CO: Westview Press, 1977.

Ury, William Langer, and Richard Smoke. *Beyond the Hotline: Controlling a Nuclear Crisis.* Cambridge, MA: Harvard Law School, 1984.

Usdin, Gene, ed. *Perspectives on Violence.* New York: Brunner/Mazel, 1972.

Utgoff, Victor A. *The Challenge of Chemical Weapons: An American Perspective.* Basingstoke, UK: Macmillan, 1990.

———. *The Coming Crisis: Nuclear Proliferation, U.S. Interests, and World Order.* Cambridge, MA: MIT Press, 2000.

VanDeMark, Brian. *Pandora's Keepers: Nine Men and the Atomic Bomb.* Boston: Back Bay Books, 2003.

Walker, J. Samuel. *Prompt and Utter Destruction: Truman and the Use of*

Atomic Bombs Against Japan. Rev. ed. Chapel Hill: University of North Carolina Press, 2004.

Walker, William. *A Perpetual Menace: Nuclear Weapons and International Order.* New York: Routledge, 2012.

Walzer, Michael. *Arguing About War.* New Haven, CT: Yale University Press, 2004.

———. *Just and Unjust Wars: A Moral Argument with Historical Illustrations.* New York: Basic Books, 1977.

———. "Political Action: The Problem of Dirty Hands." *Philosophy and Public Affairs* 2, no. 2 (1973): 160–80.

Weapons of Mass Destruction Commission. *Weapons of Terror: Freeing the World of Nuclear, Biological, and Chemical Arms.* Stockholm: Fritzes, 2006.

Weber, Eugen. *Apocalypses: Prophecies, Cults, and Millennial Beliefs Through the Ages.* Cambridge, MA: Harvard University Press, 1999.

Wedgwood, C. V. *The Thirty Years War.* New York: New York Review of Books Classics, 2005.

Weeks, Jessica L. "Autocratic Audience Costs: Regime Type and Signaling Resolve." *International Organization* 62 (2008): 35–64.

Weinberg, Steven. *Lake Views: This World and the Universe.* Cambridge, MA: Belknap Press of Harvard University Press, 2009.

Welch, David A., and James G. Blight. "The Eleventh Hour of the Cuban Missile Crisis: An Introduction to the ExComm Transcripts." *International Security* 12, no. 3 (1987): 5–92.

Wertheimer, Alan. *Coercion.* Princeton, NJ: Princeton University Press, 1987.

Whalen, Richard J. *Catch the Falling Flag: A Republican's Challenge to His Party.* Boston: Houghton Mifflin, 1972.

"White House Tapes and Minutes of the Cuban Missile Crisis." *International Security* 10, no. 1 (1985): 164–203.

Whitfield, Stephen J. *The Culture of the Cold War.* Baltimore: Johns Hopkins University Press, 1991.

Wills, Garry. *Bomb Power: The Modern Presidency and the National Security State.* New York: Penguin Press, 2010.

Wilson, Peter H. *The Thirty Years War: Europe's Tragedy.* Cambridge, MA: Belknap Press of Harvard University Press, 2009.

Wittgenstein, Ludwig. *Philosophical Investigations.* Translated by G.E.M. Anscombe. New York: Macmillan, 1958.

Wojcik, Daniel. "Embracing Doomsday: Faith, Fatalism, and Apocalyptic Beliefs in the Nuclear Age." *Western Folklore* 55, no. 4 (1996): 297–330.

———. *The End of the World As We Know It: Faith, Fatalism, and Apocalypse in America.* New York: New York University Press, 1997.

Wolfenstein, Martha. *Disaster: A Psychological Essay.* New York: Free Press, 1957.

Wolter, Detlev. *Common Security in Outer Space and International Law.* Geneva: United Nations Publications, 2006.

Wuthnow, Robert. *Be Very Afraid: The Cultural Response to Terror, Pandemics, Environmental Devastation, Nuclear Annihilation, and Other Threats.* New York: Oxford University Press, 2010.

Wyden, Peter. *Day One: Before Hiroshima and After.* New York: Simon and Schuster, 1984.

Yale, Wesley W., I. D. White, and Hasso E. von Manteuffel. *Alternative to Armageddon: The Peace Potential of Lightning War.* New Brunswick, NJ: Rutgers University Press, 1970.

Younger, Stephen M. *The Bomb: A New History.* New York: Ecco, 2010.

Yuan, Jing-dong. "Chinese Perceptions of the Utility of Nuclear Weapons: Prospects and Potential Problems in Disarmament." *Proliferation Papers* 34 (Spring 2010).

Zeman, Scott C., and Michael A. Amundson. *Atomic Culture: How We Learned to Stop Worrying and Love the Bomb.* Boulder: University Press of Colorado, 2004.

Zinn, Howard. *The Bomb.* San Francisco: City Lights Books, 2010.

Zuckerman, Edward. *The Day After World War III: The U.S. Government's Plans for Surviving a Nuclear War.* New York: Viking Press, 1984.

Zuckerman, Solly. *Nuclear Illusion and Reality.* New York: Vintage Books, 1982.

INDEX